T0116765

Little is Much When God Is In It

Do not despise these small beginnings
For the Lord rejoices to see the work begin.
Zechariah 4:10 NLT

Mrs. Barbara Jones
2764 Hwy 51 South
Lula, GA 30554

Order this book online at www.trafford.com
or email orders@trafford.com

Most Trafford titles are also available at major online book retailers.

Printed in the United States of America.

ISBN: 978-1-4269-9121-9 (sc)
ISBN: 978-1-4269-9122-6 (e)

Trafford rev. 09/28/2011

 www.trafford.com

North America & international
toll-free: 1 888 232 4444 (USA & Canada)
phone: 250 383 6864 ♦ fax: 812 355 4082

To:

From:

Date:

Note:

This book is dedicated to:

First and foremost, this book is dedicated to GOD who performed a miracle on my body!

This book is dedicated to my husband of 45 years, Troy. By the grace of God, I love you!!! You have loved me through all the ups and the downs. Thank you from the bottom of my heart. You are a wonderful man. You have helped me in more ways than I can even think about. From putting all my 15 different pills in the containers for me every day to all the times you had to drive me to the various doctors' offices; my heart goes out to you always. Praise God that he put us together; little is much when God is in it.

This book is dedicated to Tondra Boswell; my first born daughter, the one I turn to when trouble starts. Thank you for everything you have done for me during your life. You remind me that Jesus can handle everything! We just have to turn it over to Him. I just want to say thank you for standing beside me; it comes from the bottom of my heart. Thank you for all your assistance with this book. I love you all, Tondra,Rob, Gatlin, Stetson, Channing, and Canyon.

This book is dedicated to my daughter, Rhonda Thomas. Thank you for quitting your job to take care of me; little is much when God is in it. You have treasures laid up in Heaven, you have gone above and beyond "and my blessings are with you". Thank you for believing in me and for your trust in Jesus our Savior. I love you, Rhonda, Scott, Levi and Devin. Thank you for your assistance with this book.

This book is dedicated to all of my friends and family at Mt. Carmel Baptist Church. Also, my pastors at Mt. Carmel: Rev. Ralph O. and Sister Ruby Smith, who was the pastor during the time of my illness and Rev. James and Sister Sandra Duncan, my current pastor and wife.

This book is dedicated Sister Sue Worley, The Seekers Sunday School Class, and all my friends that I worked with at the Banks County Courthouse, and to my friend, Peggy Peoples, former secretary of the Stephens County Extension Service of the University of Georgia.

Introduction

My heart overflows with a good theme; my tongue is the pen of a ready writer.

PSALM 45: l NASB

Praises to the glory of God! It is because of Him that I have written this book. I want to share with others what God has done in my life and what He can do in yours. This is a powerful book about forgiveness, obedience, grace and healing. It is a beautiful depiction of how loving God and loving others can bring you to Christ. I am a miracle of the Lord Jesus Christ. Praise the Lord! I want to spend eternity with Jesus, Son of God, who was nailed to that old rugged cross and crucified. Jesus, He will never leave us nor forsake us. Dear Jesus, I'm so sorry that you suffered for my sin.

Finish what you start; God will be more impressed by what you finish.

Jesus has been my instructor with divine grace; this is a book about my life. I began this book back in 1968; without the knowledge of what God had laid out for me in the future. Later in my life, I would pray, almost every night, talking to Jesus. He is my best friend. I would get ready for bed and sleep for a while only to be awakened to a thought in my head that had to be written down. I would sleep for a few more hours, get up, and jot down more notes. I would gather up the notes every night. God was trying to tell me something and Jesus was my instructor.

God has given me a spirit of divine love all my life. I knew from the time my Mother and Father conceived me that God was in me.

Just as a newborn baby, so is God's love. I know that God is in my life every minute, every hour and every day! I didn't realize it before my illness, but God knew exactly what was going to happen to me, when it was going to happen and where it was going to happen. He handled it with His divine spirit and His righteousness.

God planned my life this way, it was not my time to die. I am so thankful for God's help because I have a lot of things to say and do. Lord, remind me how brief my time is on this earth, remind me that my days are numbered, and that my life is fleeting away. I am here on this earth for just a little while.

TO SHARE THE GOOD NEWS, CHRIST IS ALIVE!

In the beginning.....

**Gene, Barbara, Carolyn, Mom & Dad
(Ida Mae & Fletcher)**

I want to begin this book with some childhood memories. The fond memories that I will share with you took place at the house on the cover of this book. The characters represent my mama, daddy, brother, sister (in the swing), and myself.

When I was two or three years old, my Daddy, William Fletcher Poole, would go to the fields to hoe and pick cotton. He would put a sheet on the ground and tie another sheet to a tree branch to make a shade. He would leave me on the sheet while he worked. He always left me with water and food. He would check on me when he came to the end of every row or two.

When I was six or seven years old, I remember hiding behind the bed with a pan of water and a book of matches. I began to strike the matches just to enjoy the smell of the sulfur. I would drop the matches into the water to watch them float around. My Daddy missed me and began to call me," Barbara, Barbara". When I heard his voice, I was literally scared to death. He found me and told me that what I was doing was very dangerous and I could have burned down the house. Daddy, a sweet, wonderful person, gave me a whipping with a belt. He sat down and cried because he had to whip his baby girl so hard. Daddy died with lung cancer in 1982.

I can always remember my mama's warning to stop whatever I was doing. When she would clear her throat I always knew that was my cue to stop. Church was her favorite place to do this, it didn't happen often but I knew she meant business.

I can remember when I was about 12 years old and my mother kept telling me to go upstairs and bring her some canning jars. She was canning green beans or tomatoes. I just kept saying "in a minute". But finally, Mother walked over to me and slapped the fire (or "far" as we say) out of me. She said "Go upstairs and gets those jars, before I get really mad". I immediately went up stairs and got the jars.

Mama was always sewing for me. She made me wool skirts every fall; beautiful light blue, pink, yellow, and mint green and I had sweaters to match each outfit. She made most everything I wore to school except for my blouses and sweaters. I will never forget when Troy asked me to the Junior-Senior prom. Mama made me a long, fitted pink satin dress. I felt that it looked beautiful on me.

It was a beautiful, spring day when my mother called to me at 6:30 a.m. "Hurry up and get ready for school". It was always such a hassle for me to get up, get dressed and go over to my neighbor's house to meet the school bus. I would always wait until I got to the Wilson's house to put on my make-up and comb my hair. It seemed like it was always such a long wait until the bus would come by to pick me up. Mr. Olin Pruitt was my bus driver.

My dad was a carpenter and had to begin work at 7:30 a.m. My mother was the manager of McConnell's 5 & 10 cents store. Her job began at 9:00 a.m. but she did not drive. My Dad would take my mother to my cousin's house in Commerce where she had a long wait before she walked up town to her job. My mother knew these arrangements were hard for all of us.

My mother was raised by her mother with a faith in God and passed it on to us. I remember my Grandmother, Nancy Camilla Massey. She had long brown hair that she kept in a little ball with a hair-pin down at the back of her head. She was always sitting in her rocking chair rocking and reading the words of Jesus Christ our Savior from her Bible. My Mama passed away in 1999, thank you Jesus for giving me a loving Mother. She was always there for me every time I needed her. John 14:3 says that "Where I am, ye may be also". I know that I will see her again in heaven.

My brother, Gene Poole, who was 10 years older than me, used to chase me to the top of the hill in front of our house. He was trying to catch me and make me get in the stack of stove wood. At that time, we had to cook on a wood-burning stove. He was always mean to me, or that is what I thought. He even tied tin cans with rocks in them to my pet dog's tail. When his buddies would come over, he would shoot a rifle into the air. This would scare my dog to death. The dog would run, barking, up the road. My brother and his buddies would laugh and laugh and laugh. I loved my brother Gene. I regret to say he passed away in 2001.

My sister was always good to me and I'll never forget the day she got married. I was about thirteen years old and I truly hated the man she was marrying because I thought he was taking my sister away from me. In 2010, God blessed my sister and her husband with 50 years of marriage. I learned to love my brother-in-law! Ha!!!!

My family attended Webb's Creek Baptist Church. Mother never asked if we wanted to go to church; if we weren't sick, we knew that we were to get up and get ready to go to church on Sunday morning, Sunday night, and Wednesday night. We also attended most all of the other events that were held at our church.

Once when it was revival time at Webb's Creek in 1957 and I was about nine years old, this elderly lady came up to me and told me that Johnnie, Sandra, and Brenda came up that night to join the church. She stated that she kept waiting for me to come up. I said, "Oh, I thought I was too young". On Thursday night I finally went to the front of the church. I told them I was saved. I was baptized in Toney's Lake (a place where everyone who joined the church was baptized). God was very important to me and I knew right from wrong.

When I was fourteen years old I was still a pretty small size. I had medium length, sandy blond hair and was 5 feet 3 inches tall. I attended Banks County School and was in the eighth grade. I enjoyed school life and made lots of friends. I made the most of every day and almost always accomplished what I set out to do.

Mom allowed me to participate in parties, sports and have friends come over for visits. I could basically do what I wanted as long as I behaved myself in a way that could be counted as trustworthy. I believed Mom meant every word she said. As I look back today, I really believe she would have been proud of me when I was not in her sight.

My parents had brought me up to do unto your neighbor, as you would have him to do unto you. I always tried to be nice to everyone no matter who they were. I just smiled and spoke to everyone. My friends who were less fortunate were just as much my friends as any of them. I remember one day when there was a friend of mine that never got to eat in the lunchroom. I ate her buttered biscuits and I let her take my place in the lunch line.

Don't get me wrong, we didn't have a lot but Mother would do without so I could have what I wanted. Mother saw to it that I always had lunch money. She always made sure that I had the most stylish clothes to wear from black and white saddle oxfords to a black leather jacket and John Romaine pocketbook. (See, I told you that I was spoiled; even if I didn't know it at that time).

There were six girls that hung around together; Myra (my best friend), Gaynell, Brenda, Kitty, Carolyn and me. I remember spending the night at Gaynell's with all the girls. We laughed and giggled until 2 a.m. Gaynell said "Please be quiet because my dad has an ulcer". At 3 am: "Shh...shh... Elzie has an ulcer". We would giggle and giggle, not that we were laughing at Mr. Pritchett having an ulcer, but because to a bunch of young girls, everything was funny at that time of night.

Kitty Lou, Myra, Barbara, Gaynell

Barbara in Jeans, with her first grade friends

When I was in about the 5th or 6th grade I spent the night with Carolyn. Her mother said, "I'll fix you some breakfast". She prepared gravy and loaf bread with a banana beside the plate. We sat down to a beautiful breakfast. Carolyn picked up her banana and her fork and began mashing the banana on her plate. She put her loaf bread on top and poured gravy over it. Carolyn said, "It's delicious." I said, "No thanks, I think I will take my banana to school for a snack".

My family's farmhouse was down a dirt road with no houses around. When we would spend the night at my house all of us girls usually slept upstairs. After the lights had to be turned off, someone would say they heard a noise. We would get scared, giggle, and talk really loudly. Usually, Mom would come upstairs to check on us. This one time she tried to tell us there was nothing to be afraid of and then she went back downstairs. We didn't go to sleep though and the giggling just got louder. Finally, she came back upstairs, and lay down with us so that we would go to sleep. After all, we had to get up and go to school the next morning.

In school, break time was the best. I would buy a pack of crackers and a Coke and share with all the girls. We each got one cracker and a couple of swigs of Coke. We girls did not think anything about germs; we were just glad to get some snack food! I always tried to be generous with whatever I had; my mom taught me that. We always laughed a lot and had some very happy times together at school.

I was in Mrs. Miller's 8th grade class which was always lots of fun. She was my teacher in 7th grade, also. When the school had to create another 8th grade class, she applied for the job and moved up to teach that class and it was the only 8th grade class in Banks Co. High school. Our class was excited because she was a wonderful teacher. It was very evident that the love between Mrs. Miller and her class was mutual.

When the weather got warm outside, Mrs. Miller would let us go to the baseball field and play softball. I wasn't much for playing ball but this gave me the chance to see this new guy, Troy Jones. Every one of the girls were just dying to meet him. Gaynell had already put dubs on him. To me, there was just something special about this new fellow. More about him later…

The 9th grade was one of the most exciting of my teenage years. Myra, my best friend and I did everything together. We had parties galore. Most of them were held at the American Legion Building (a place in our town that you could rent for parties and gatherings) with lots of chaperones of course. We planned the parties for Monday or Thursday evenings, Wednesday evening was church and Tuesday and Friday were ballgame nights. On Friday, Saturday, and Sunday nights we usually dated. On Sunday nights our dates attended church with us. We would often triple date. Sounds like a full calendar.

My 9th grade year became one of the most memorable years of my life. I remember it was time to elect our Homecoming Queen. I was elected to be on the Homecoming court but never expected to win, I was only a freshman. I was overwhelmed when my name, Barbara Poole, was called out as Homecoming Queen. This was the first time that a ninth grader was elected as Miss Banks County Homecoming Queen. All of the teachers were concerned about the fact that the Queen was supposed to be a senior. The year following my reign, the teachers created rules and guidelines so there would be a representative from each grade level and the Homecoming Queen would be elected from the senior contestants only.

Next came the Miss Princess of Hearts contest (for 9th and 10th graders) and I started working hard on my modeling, walking, turning, and smiling. I had no idea that I even had a chance in the world to win. Mom bought me the most beautiful mint green dress to wear. I chose Jack Carlan from Commerce High School to be my escort. I thought Gaynell would win because of her poise and gracefulness. When my name was called out, I was so shocked! I thought they wanted me to do something else - I couldn't believe I had won the Banks County Princess of Hearts Contest!

And now for a little more about the guy named Troy that I mentioned before. At this time, Gaynell was dating Troy and I was going out with Randall, Troy's best friend, and Myra was dating William, another friend of Troy and Randall's. Those dating years were some of the funniest days of our lives. Myra and I were mature for our age. Most of the boys that we dated with the exception of a few were older. We did not want most of the younger guys for boyfriends because they were immature or at least that is what we thought. Although, I must say that all of the guys in our class were my friends and I was nice to everyone.

The things that we did back then were very different from what teenagers do now for fun. We would ride down thrill hill, throw Mr. Wilson's apples at signs or steal a watermelon from someone's patch. Most of the guys would occasionally try to smoke a cigarette or two. When we were coming up, drugs and alcohol were not as much of an issue as it is today. There wasn't as much drinking back then with the teenagers, the guys would have been afraid to go home drunk because there would be a big, black leather strap waiting for them! We either were afraid that if we did things that we shouldn't, our parents would find out or we would be looked at as being with the rough crowd. Most of our parents had us under their fingernail and we knew better than to get into trouble.

Sometimes we three couples would go to the Old Cornelia Drive Inn. At this time Myra knew that I did not like Randall as a boyfriend. Myra and I both liked Troy. It seemed that everyone liked Troy. I'll never forget the six of us in the car the first night we triple dated. I was in the front seat with Randall. Gaynell, Troy, Myra, and William were all in the back seat. I kept hearing Gaynell telling Troy "No". Myra told me later that Troy tried to kiss Gaynell and she would not let him. A few weeks later Gaynell and Troy broke up (little did everyone know but I was really happy about it).

A few weeks after the break up, Troy asked Myra out. Gaynell sort of drifted from the picture. It really didn't matter to her because she didn't like Troy anyway. She stated to the rest of us that he was not her type. Of course, I knew that, but still I could not seem to get him out of my mind. I would go out with Randall, Troy and Myra just to be around him. At that time I was 15 years old, in the 9th grade and was falling head over heels in love with Troy.

Myra and Troy just kept dating. I didn't try to break them up but I really wanted to go out with him. I continued to date Randall and some other guys from Banks and Jackson County. I dated some of the most popular guys including the captain of the football teams, all the while, it drove me crazy to see Myra with Troy. It didn't matter though because Troy and I were total opposites and he did not like me in the least. This didn't stop me and I began planning my strategy, setting out like a snake in the grass getting ready to strike. It did not matter whether or not they were going steady I just wanted to be around him. I spent a lot of time at Myra's house, double dated with them, and was kept informed by Myra. Most of the time I knew during the day what Troy was going to do that night. If I knew the regular gang was going to be somewhere then chances were Troy might be there, I would make plans to be there always trying to look my best.

One day out of nowhere, Myra said to me, "Barbara don't get mad at me but I've got something to tell you," All the time I was scared to death thinking that she and Troy were getting married or something. I said to Myra "What is it?" She said, "I want to go out with Randall". I told her that it was fine with me that I didn't have a problem with this. In fact, I had never been so glad to hear anything in all my life. "Hope it works out for you!" All of the other girls were after Troy as soon as he and Myra broke up. As I stated before, he couldn't stand me. Even though I was pretty and popular, I was a flirt and talked to everyone. I was friendly to all of the boys but I obviously was not Troy's type. Slowly but surely as the year was coming to an end, I began to notice a change in Troy's attitude. I just played it cool and did not push the issue. I was secretly watching him like a hawk, following his every move. I know this sounds terrible, but I had to have him.

One day during final exams, the bell rang and I was in a hurry to get to the next class. Someone walked up behind me and said "Hey, wait a minute!" Of all people, it was Troy. He said "What are you doing this weekend?" My heart did a double flip and almost stopped. I replied, "Oh, nothing. Why?" He said that he, Mike, and Trudy (two of Troy's friends) were thinking about going to Lake Spivey in Atlanta. He wondered if I would like to go with them. I could hardly speak! I told him "Yes, I guess. What time will you be leaving?" He said they would pick me up around 9:00 am. I thought that I would absolutely die. I went to Mr. Bass's room for a test and of course, I failed it. There was no way I could concentrate; Troy had just asked me out for heaven's sake! As I said before, Troy did not like me because he thought I was a flirt and loudmouth, but I think he felt that same funny feeling in his stomach that I did whether he wanted to admit it or not.

William Troy Jones & Barbara Ann Poole "The Couple"

This was the happiest day of my life, I finally had a date with the most popular, best looking, voted cutest guy in Banks County High School. I was going to have a ball and show Troy I was everything he thought I wasn't. I just wanted him to see what he was missing. Saturday dawned bright and beautiful...nothing could be wrong! It was my first date with "Mr. Right" and boy was I ever nervous! I had been working up to this for the past two years. What else could I ask for? I knew that I could not bum this up.

When we arrived at Lake Spivey, the guys went on down to the beach while Trudy and I went to the beach house to put on our swimsuits. Trudy came out in a slim two piece swimsuit. Mom had a sister that worked in Athens at Macy's. She had bought me a swanky one-piece swimsuit. The suit fit well and I thought that I was stylish and pretty. So what did I have to worry about? Plenty...

My heart turned a couple of flips when I saw Troy spreading out beach towels for us. I was thinking that this was the most handsome sight my eyes could ever see. When Trudy and I walked down to where the guys were, I had this funny feeling in my stomach. As I lay down on the towel next to him, my heart pounding, I kept trying to make conversation. Thank goodness that Mike and Trudy were there. Trudy and Mike were two years older than Troy. Troy was two years older than I was. Mike and Troy were always kidding each other or joking about something making the atmosphere a little more relaxed. Everything was going well until I got into the water. My lovely yellow floral swimsuit ballooned into a big yellow blimp. I was so embarrassed!

When we got back to my house it was late afternoon, Troy got out, walked me to the door and kissed me in a way I had never been kissed before. He told me he had a great time, he would see me at school on Monday and said good-night.

I went in the house but no one was there. Mother was still at work. She worked from 9 am to 6 pm every Saturday. I went to my room, lay on the bed and replayed the date through my mind over and over. It was perfect; I was so happy. I felt like I worshiped the ground that Troy walked on. As I sat on my bed, I looked in the mirror across the room. I thought that I looked terrible. So, I got up to have a closer look. Oh my goodness!!! Evidently my lipstick had turned solid white. It looked sickening and Troy had kissed me! I could have just died!!! Oh, I thought, he will never ask me out or have anything else to do with me. Between my swimsuit fiasco and me looking like a ghost, I didn't think he would ever talk to me again. I cried like a baby!

On Monday, I arrived at school before 8:00 a.m. I wasn't sure if Troy would meet me, talk to me, eat lunch with me or even act as if I existed. Sure enough, just as I thought, he didn't have much to say. It was just as if the date was nothing special. Monday through Thursday he only spoke to me when we would pass each other in the hallway. I was thinking that if he didn't ask me out by Friday, I would just die. I can remember that Friday as if it were yesterday, I had chosen a light blue skirt with a white button down shirt, loafers and hose to wear. My outfit looked good and fit very well.

That afternoon we had an assembly. As Myra and I were going out to the gym, there were Troy and Randall waiting outside the school door. Myra knew that Randall would sit with her as they had been dating for some time. We all walked in together but I had no idea if Troy would sit with me or not. I felt like a star when we walked in and he sat down beside me. We laughed and talked with the people around us. Randall asked "Why don't we all go somewhere tomorrow night?" My cheeks got bright red due to the fact that Troy had not said anything about us going out. Troy said, "Sure, we would if you want to—we'll talk about it." Well, no one mentioned Friday night because it was a basketball game. It just so happened that the game was a home game, which was good for me. Since Mother did not drive and Father went to bed early, during the day Myra and I made our plans for me to go home with her after school. We would go to the ballgame later. All the time, we were hoping that Randall and Troy would ask to take us home. Randall played basketball and always took Myra home after the games. Myra told Randall that I was going home with her after the game. She told him that if he wanted to ask Troy to come over it would be fine. So it worked out just like we planned! We went to Cornelia Dairy Queen and we all got something to eat. Afterwards we went to Myra's house, sat around, watched TV and talked. I was the happiest person in the world (again) because Troy had made me that way.

The following Saturday I was supposed to have a date with Leon, a very popular, good-looking guy from Commerce High School (our rival school). Leon worked at one of the nearby men's stores in town. I was at work with my mother that morning. Only by fate, I called him early that Saturday and told him my parents were going out of town and I was going to have to cancel my date that evening because they were making me go with them. One of the other guys that worked there came over to the snack bar and said that Leon was sick because I had cancelled our date. I really put on the dog about my parents making me go with them because I liked Leon, but not as much or the same way as I did Troy.

Later that evening, as I sat in the swing that Saturday afternoon, a beautiful sunset was coming up at the back of the ridge, just over the hill. I did not have a telephone and had not talked with Troy. I had seen him at the basketball game the night before and caught him looking at me a couple of times. I sat there sad and lonely for Troy. I just wanted to see him, to touch him and to kiss him because I knew I loved him deeply with all my heart. What a beautiful sight to behold because there came Troy over the hill in his red and white '56 Ford. And that's how it all started.

Troy was a romantic but he was also very much a gentleman. He had all the qualities I ever needed in a man. After we dated a few months, I realized that Troy was quite a jealous guy. He didn't want me to to look at another guy. Therefore, we would be together for a month or two and then break up for a few weeks because Troy was mad at me.

So at school, I became very cool to most of the boys except to speak to them. I was friendly and outgoing – that was just my personality. But I had lots of friends from the nearby town, Commerce. When I was down there, I didn't have to worry about Troy finding out. I tried to be very careful. You see, I wanted to have my cake and eat it, too.

Whether boy or girl, he could not adjust to my talking to everyone so we broke up quite a few more times. Most of the time, Troy had a real temper. If he got mad there was no talking to him.

After dating on and off for two years, Troy's behavior began to change. One night in particular, Randall, Myra, Troy and I had gone to the movies. The radio was playing *Talk Back Trembling Lips*. As long as I live, I will never forget the name of that song. I was so nervous and then it happened: Troy kissed me and he said, "I love you". I was so shocked! I knew without a doubt that Troy was serious. He knew what he saying to me meant spending a lifetime together they were not just words. I was seventeen and he was nineteen years old. I was so much in love with Troy.... Troy was the light of my life. One happy moment, Praise God!

The Wedding....

Therefore shall a man leave his father and his mother, and shall cleave unto his wife: and they shall be one flesh.

Genesis 2:24KJV

We announced our wedding to be held July 10, 1965 at 7:30 pm at Webb's Creek Baptist Church. Myra would be my matron of honor, Troy's sister, Kathy, and my sister would be my bridesmaids. Mike Galloway would be the best man. Willard (a friend of Troy's) and my brother-in-law Hugh were ushers. Trudy would keep the bride's book and Gaynell would sing "Wherever Thou Go'est I Will Go". It was perfect; just like I had dreamed.

Mr. & Mrs. William Troy Jones

And Ruth said, Entreat me not to leave thee, or to return from following after thee: for whither thou go'est, I will go; and where thou lodgest, I will lodge: thy people shall be my people, and thy God my God:

Ruth 1:16 KJV

After our honeymoon we returned home to a little white house we had rented behind Pruitt's Grocery in Homer. It belonged to Troy's Aunt Gladys and Uncle Clyde. We stayed there for about nine months. I think the rent was $25.00 per month.

Back then, Troy had to get up at 4:00 am to go to work. I remember ironing and starching his white long sleeve shirts every Wednesday afternoon, because that was the day I was off of work. Troy worked at Preformed Line Products in Atlanta making $1.65 per hour. Troy rode to work with Joe Hill and they took turns driving. I didn't have my driver's license at that time so Troy would have to take me to my parent's house where I would ride with my daddy to work in Commerce. I worked as a sales clerk at Commerce Jewelry. Mr. Watt, the owner, paid me $35.00 a week. I was a good sales clerk and Mr. Watts once told me, "You could sell your shoes right off your feet". I worked for him about five years.

The little house we lived in wasn't much and it didn't take us long until we had had enough. One night when Troy and I returned home from work, I pulled the string to turn on the light and there was a huge rat (in the south we call them "Warf-rat") sitting between my feet. I was terrified of rats. I was scared to death and like to have died. Later that same night I heard Troy calling me as he was turning back the sheets. I ran to see what was wrong. There was a rat in the bed and I screamed. The next day Troy talked with his dad and told him we were going to build a house; he had had enough. We were approved for our loan and Troy and his dad began building our home.

We built our house next door to Horace and Rosie, Troy's parents. Troy's family owned Jones Trophy Shop; it was between our house and his parent's house. He had a younger sister, Kathy and brother Wayne, both still living at home. Troy and I didn't have a lot of extra money but his family treated me like one of them and every time Horace sent Kathy and Rosie to town to buy a new dress he made sure I got one, too. I was just like one of his kids.

I remember another time when Horace helped me get my favorite car ever. It was a 1969 Malibu Super Sport, black and gray, so sharp! It was for sale in Commerce and I wanted it badly. Troy went to look at it and he thought it was a good car and a good deal but we couldn't afford it. Troy argued the car down to $1,500.00. It was a lot of money back in the seventies. Horace knew how badly I wanted that car and he gave us the extra $500.00 so we could get the car. It was a beauty and I loved it.

I can remember when Troy and I first married. I was only 17 years old and everything was sugar and spice. Then...the real life began and our family began to grow and grow. Only now, I can say how important it is to stay married.

Thank you, Troy, for not letting me leave when I would get so mad. We wouldn't sit down and talk about the problem as God expects us to do. Things are different now!

You always have Jesus, my best friend, to talk to about anything. Jesus is waiting on you, to knock, to seek, and Jesus will be there (Matthew 7:7-8 KJV). As the Bible tells us, God will never leave us, nor forsake us.

Troy and I celebrated forty-five years together in 2010.

Barbara & Troy

*Love is looking
outward together in
the same direction*

BJ's Children Shoppe 1979

Barbara & Troy 1991

And then there were four...

Troy and I had been married for four years, I was 21 and Troy was 23. We had talked about having a baby. In 1968, I was examined by Dr. Holloway and discovered what I suspected was true: I was going to have a baby. Troy and I were so happy. During my first month things seemed to be going well but then I began to have complications. It became worse when I was about 3½ months into my pregnancy. I woke one morning and told Troy something was very wrong. Troy called Dr. Holloway who told him to get me to the hospital as soon as possible. I was rushed to Banks-Jackson-Commerce Hospital. When I woke up, I cried when the nurses told me I had a miscarriage. I had lost my baby, something that God had given me. I felt sick to my stomach.

A couple of years later, Tondra Lynn was born on January 13, 1970 during a terrible ice storm. We had stayed at my sister's house behind the hospital just in case there was an emergency. Troy had to ride the lawnmower up and down the driveway just so we could get up the hill because of all the ice. Thank you Jesus!! I had finally done it. I found myself in hard labor pain for 5 days and nights and would scream with each pain. It was a very hard delivery as she was born breech. She weighed 7 lbs. 9 oz and was such a beautiful baby girl. Tondra had features just like her Father and he was so happy. She had brown hair and brown eyes and was named after her Aunt Kathy Lynn. All our neighbors came to see Tondra.

Our first trip to church with Tondra was when she was just about 10 weeks old. We went to Gillsville Baptist Church with Marie Gardiner a neighbor who lived across the street from us. Then as time went on, Greg and Chris, Marie's boys, Tondra and myself, would go to Sunday School. At night, Troy and Roy (Marie's husband) would come to preaching services. I went to church with Marie for about five years.

During this time Troy's brother Wayne was serving in Vietnam. Troy's parents had a huge reel to reel tape recorder that they used to send tapes back and forth to Wayne. I especially remember recording Tondra's coos and goo's and sending them to him. When Wayne came home she was about 6 months old and he spoiled her rotten.

Tondra wasn't even a year old when I went to see Dr. Holloway again. I'll never forget what he said; he just looked at me and said "You had better not be", but he was wrong, I was pregnant with my second baby! During that time, we did not have sonograms to determine the baby's sex. On March 17, 1972, my second daughter was born. Her name was Rhonda Leigh; she weighed 8 lbs 10 oz and was also born breech. Rhonda looked just like me. She had blond hair and beautiful blue eyes inherited from my father, William Fletcher Poole.

Barbara & Troy with the girls, Tondra Lynn and Rhonda Leigh

The growing up years...

Looking back, our lives seem to be filled with incident after incident where God was watching out for us.

In 1973, when Rhonda was just a baby, we were with Kathy coming home from town. Tondra was standing in the front seat and I was holding Rhonda. Car seats were not legally required and were rarely used at the time. We ran off the shoulder of the road and hit a tree. Thank God for that tree because there was a huge drop off just on the other side. Tondra's head hit the windshield and she had some scrapes. Rhonda seemed to be fine but later that night she would not stop crying. She had cried for hours and hours and nothing would help. We finally had to take her to the emergency room and they had to pump her stomach. She had just eaten before the wreck and had not digested the bottle. Other than that everyone was fine, and we were very blessed!

When Rhonda was 15 months old, I had borrowed Rosie's car. I pulled into the driveway and parked. Rhonda came out of the house and was walking down the driveway at the same time the car began to roll backward. For some reason Rhonda laid down in the driveway and the car rolled over her legs. We took her to the emergency room but she had no broken bones! The doctors said her bones were so flexible that nothing broke. Another blessing!

One afternoon Tondra was sitting on the front porch of Horace and Rosie's house with Kathy while their cousin, Steve, was cutting grass. Steve ran over part of a brick and it flew from under the lawnmower and hit Tondra on the knee. We were at the Trophy Shop working when we heard the screaming. We put her in the car and took her to Northeast Georgia Medical Center. She had over 100 stitches in her little tiny leg and a cast all the way to her hip; she had to scoot everywhere she went for weeks. The doctors said it was by the Grace of God that she did not lose her leg.

Tondra & Rhonda after the lawn mower accident

When the girls were a little older, they were sick with a terrible cough and no matter what Dr. Newman gave them it wouldn't stop. Eventually, they were hospitalized, both in the same room. Finally Dr. Newman figured out what was wrong with them, they had whopping cough and had to be quarantined. We had to wear scrubs to go in to see them and their sheets had to be put in special containers. Once the girls were feeling better they enjoyed the attention.

Rhonda and Tondra in dresses made by Maw-Maw Poole

When the girls were about two and four years old we began attending Mt. Carmel Baptist Church. I joined Mt. Carmel not realizing I had really not accepted the Lord as my Savior. Our pastor, Rev. Ralph O. Smith, would preach and I'd go to the altar a lot. One day as Brother Smith was preaching, I felt the Holy Spirit come over me like I'd never known before. I was sitting on the second pew listening to the choir singing *Jesus is Right for Whatever is Wrong in Your Life*. I told Brother Smith that I had never been saved. I realized that I was a sinner, and Brother Smith prayed with me as I asked God to save me. A few weeks later I was baptized.

I worked many jobs over the years from sales clerk to owning my own children's clothing shop. I had a business in Commerce called *B.J.'s Children's Shoppe*. I had a real love for children and loved my job but everything wasn't perfect. One day a man from my church stopped by my shop to bring some dolls for me to sell. There I was, puffin' away on a cancer stick. I had smoked for 17 years. I had tried to stop many times but each time I failed. I really didn't see the seriousness of it at the time. But this day was different. He looked me at me and said "B.J. why don't you stop smoking those nasty things." I explained that I really wanted to but just had not been able to find the strength to do so. "I love'em so much I could chew them up." He looked me straight in the eye and said "Well, you're going to kill your kids" and he left.

His words hit me like a rock! I laid them down that minute and began praying for God to give me strength. Over and over lots of times each day I would pray and repeat: *I can do all things through Christ who strengthens me. (Philippians 4:13 KJV)* I thank God for sending my friend that day. His words were like a sharp knife that cut straight to my heart. Nothing was more important in my life than Troy and my two beautiful girls. I never smoked again after that day. Praise God!

As teenagers, the girls were both pretty well behaved. If I have to choose one, it was Rhonda that pushed the limits more. Her room was always a terrible mess. When Tondra and Rhonda were younger, Tondra would clean Rhonda's room so she would not get in trouble. I guess she got tired of doing that because as a teenager you could not even walk through it. We had many, many "discussions" (screaming battles) about it but one day her daddy walked by and just closed the door. "If she is going to live like that, I'm not going to look at it." It's really ironic because today Rhonda is an immaculate housekeeper!

When Rhonda was in the 10th grade she became good friends with Jennifer Crabbe and Amy Clough. At a Mt. Carmel Youth meeting, Mrs. Betty, the youth director at the time, asked if someone would lead them in a closing prayer. Rhonda spoke-up and said that she would. Rhonda prayed giving God all the Glory, the Honor, and the Praise for her life. I realized that hanging around with that group of girls was the best thing in this world for her.

Isn't it strange how in our lives our paths cross? Rhonda attended church at Gillsville Baptist Church when Levi was a small child with Rev. Charles Crabbe (Jennifer Crabbe's father) as her pastor. Rev. Crabbe is now her pastor at Homer Baptist Church where she is the director of the church preschool and works with the youth. It all goes back to the title of this book; *Little is Much When God is in It.*

Back to our story, in 1990, Troy and I purchased a 1986 Camaro for Rhonda as a combined birthday, graduation and Christmas gift. It was white with gold stripes - sporty, just like her. We took the car to Tondra's house and put a big bow on top. We called Rhonda and when she saw the car she started crying. She got down and kissed the ground and said "Thank you, Jesus". She was so excited to be 'moving up' from a 1978 Cutlass.

Adventures During Our Life....

There were three couples that we shared many adventures with through the years. William and Carolyn Carpenter who were married June 25, 1965, Mary Sue (Pia) and Billy Meeks married June 30, 1962, and Stanley and Jeanette Crocker married July 1965. We shared many vacations, trips to the mountains and beach as our children were growing up and we were growing older. We miss Stanley, in 2007; he went home to live with our Lord Jesus Christ.

I remember one Sunday afternoon before Troy and I married, the four couples went to Cherokee, North Carolina. It was hot outside and we stopped to get some cold cider. Everyone had some with no problems. On the way home, Stanley started straightening out the curves. We had to stop so William could drive. Stanley must have drunk out of the wrong kind of cider. Between the stops in the woods (no bathrooms available back then) we finally made it home that day.

I recall our 1977 vacation to Daytona Beach, Florida. Our group was made up of Troy and me, Pia and Billy, Melinda (Pia and Billy's daughter) and her friend Shelly, William and Carolyn, and their children, Chris and Angie. Audrey and Danny (relatives of Pia) came with us on their honeymoon! Each family had separate rooms. Audrey and Danny they stayed at another place down the street. After all, it was their wedding night.

We left at midnight and had our swimming gear packed in a bag to hit the beach at sun up so we wouldn't lose an ounce of sun. Troy pulled his dune buggy to Daytona Beach from Lula. What a week. We piled as many people on the dune buggy as would fit. We would hang on and ride up and down the beach. What fun! When we couldn't take anymore sun, Troy, Billy and the other guys would put up a homemade tent made of a white sheet because nobody had the money to rent a umbrella and Melinda and Shelly would move a ways down the beach from us (I wonder why?).

Our Family at the beach

Beach Friends

Our Family Grows.....

In 1987 Tondra began dating Rob Boswell. They went on their first date only because I convinced her to go. She didn't think he was her type but there was something about him. Rob had brain surgery the year before and Tondra had come to know his family. Rob and Tondra dated for about a year and one night he came to talk to Troy, he told him he loved his daughter and wanted to marry her.

On May 23, 1989, I wrote a letter to Tondra for her wedding. I would like to share it:

Dear Tondra,   July 1, 1989

I remember: when our family went out to eat at the Ponderosa and how you and Rhonda would fuss because you had to divide a steak. Betty's Beginner's Sunday school Class or Ms. Ruby's pet in Kindergarten class. How about your first date (6 years old) with Oscar, him coming to the door asking, "What time do I have to have your daughter home, Mrs. Jones?" Or in 5th grade when Mr. Bertrang gave you a spanking and it made me so mad I wanted to go pull his hair out!!! Eighth grade – Miss Banks County Elementary and eighth grade graduation... "All those beauty pageants"...and your real first dance, when Kathy took you to buy you something to wear. WOW, I'll never forget that night, you looked so great, 13 and so grown up!!! And the day you accepted Jesus as your Savior and was baptized. I was so proud of you and sort of relieved in a very special way. You're junior and senior prom, that day and night, I was so sad that day until I thought I would die. I was not about to let you know how sad I was; there you were running around, all smiles, so happy. All I could think was stay away from her and she'll never know. Then you came out with, "Well Mama you never even told me that I looked pretty." Die,

I thought I would die. I managed to come out with something and told you that you looked beautiful. I was holding back tears, thinking that my pride and joy had grown up and your sister, Rhonda, is right behind you. My babies were grown, High School Graduation. I MADE IT!!! This is the way God planned it. So we must make the best out of the time "God allows us to Share Together".

All I ask of you, Tondra, is to strive to go forward in life. You will make mistakes; just learn from them. When times get hard, don't give up, remember to pray. You have not seen, as far as eye sight, me pray very much but Tondra I talk to God often and I pray for you and Rob. I pray that the Lord will bless your marriage and that you will always allow him to be the leader of your lives together. You will never be sorry. This is one thing your mother firmly believes with all my heart. I just wish your father and I could let him closer in our home. By this, I mean prayer at mealtime and devotion at bedtime. This is very important. If you don't begin marriage with these factors, then you will never have them.

As we now have shared nineteen years together and gone through many phases of life, I love you more than you could imagine even through the last year I know has been hard. Just forgive me because I am going through a phase in my life and it's something I have no control over, flares-up's hot flashes, Ha! (And you know what; I never understood this about my mother, (until now!!!)

Well, I think you know what I am trying to say, I love you: You are special, and you'll always be my baby in a sort of way, but that's just the way mother's love is and some day, if it's God's will, you will understand.

July 1, 1989, as you have chosen your mate for life; I am very happy for you, because I know you feel the love for Rob that I felt and still do the day I married your father. However, life is not always a bundle of roses and marriage isn't either. There will be up days and down days, but if you can discuss and forgive, your real love for each other will show through. Some days you might think you won't make it, but hang in there, you will, it's just the old devil telling you that you won't.

Please remember that marriage does not succeed or fail; those who make up the marriage succeed or fail in their relationship with each other. Marriage brings two people together, but it can't give them the qualities needed to make their union succeed. If these qualities aren't present when the union if formed, the relationship is in trouble from the very start.

If both partners are mature, loving, kind, and considerate, chances are high that their marriage will succeed. If either is childish, then selfishness and strife are going to ravage their relationship from the very start. The kind of marriage you have is governed by the qualities you possess.

Tondra, do a good job with whatever you do in life. My prayers and love are with you. Where I've failed---"I'm sorry." Wherever, I have helped---I'm glad. You and I have had many long talks and learned many lessons. We'll never cease to learn. Experience is a dear teacher.

Take your time, make wise decisions. I pray you will be thankful, humble, and grateful for all that GOD has DONE FOR YOU. We have been blessed – far more than we deserve.

God Bless You,
I Love You,
Your Mother and Best Friend

I am so thankful to God for calling Rob to ministry. His first sermon was at Gillsville Baptist Church on April 26, 2009.

Soon after Tondra and Rob were married, Rhonda met her love. Scott Thomas was from Commerce and after dating for several months, Scott went to Troy to ask for his daughter's hand in marriage. They were married on December 28, 1991, at Mount

Carmel Baptist Church. It was a beautiful Christmas wedding and Tondra was her maid of honor.

Tondra & Rob Boswell

Scott & Rhonda Thomas

5 Generations, Mama Lois (troy's grandmother),
Boo Granny (Troy's mother), Rhonda, and
Levi Scott Thomas*

5 Generations- Mama Lois, Boo Granny, Troy, Tondra,
Gatlin Robert Boswell

Since this time our family has continued to grow, we have been blessed with six beautiful grandchildren. Each one of them holds a special place in our hearts.

Levi Scott Thomas was born January 4, 1994. Troy had the flu when he was born and couldn't see him until he was over a week old. He would go to Scott and Rhonda's apartment and look at Levi through the window until he was well enough to hold him. He was such a blessing. Everyone spoiled him rotten - especially his Aunt Tondra. He had more clothes than were probably in my entire clothing store. As a toddler he loved "ball shirts" and any shirt that had a ball on it. He would not wear anything else. Rhonda finally convinced him that for church he could wear his ball shirt under his church shirt and take it off as soon as church was over. I can recall another rather funny story about Levi. When he was about three years old, he was eating a hot dog. He went to the table to get another but this one he decided to hide under his bed until later. Well, *later* turned out to be weeks later. Rhonda spotted him one day walking around with a mold covered hot dog. He told her he got it from underneath his bed where he had hidden it just in case he was hungry.

Levi & Grand-Baba- His first truck!

Gatlin Robert Boswell was born January 18, 1996. I think Gatlin has been holding a ball since he was born. I can't remember a time when he was not interested in a sports of any kind and he still is today. Gatlin has always been a talker; he spoke plainly even as a toddler and talked to anyone. I remember Gatlin talking to a waitress without any prompting and saying "Hey baby." Another time he asked a little girl in a restaurant what her name was, when the little girl didn't answer he just laughed and said "She doesn't even know her name."

Gatlin shooting a foul shot, 9ᵗʰ grade JV Basketball Team

Devin Stone Thomas was born January 23, 1997. Devin has been on the go from the beginning. If someone was working on something Devin had to be there. By the age of three he could drive the lawn mover, ride a bike and he even wrecked a truck! Rob and Scott were working under the hood of Scott's truck at the barn one day and three year old Devin was in the cab. Scott had already taken the battery cable off because he knew that Devin could crank the truck himself. Devin, not being able to crank the truck decided to pulled the truck out of gear and it began rolling backward. As he rolled down the barn driveway, he stood in the cab and looked at his daddy and Rob. They began chasing the truck but it was speeding up and headed down a huge hill. The truck ran over a large log on the ground that tore most everything out from under the truck. The rear wheels went over the log, but the front would not so the truck came to a stop. The truck was totaled but Devin did not have a scratch!

Devin Stone Thomas riding his dirt bike

Stetson Troy Boswell was born October 1, 1998. Stetson is so much like his Pop in appearance and mannerism. Stetson likes to be outside, on the tractor with Pop, or feeding the cows. I feel like I missed a lot of time with Stetson when he was a baby because I was so sick from almost the time he was born. Today Stetson is happiest when he is fishing or hunting. In 2010 he shot his first deer and caught a 9 pound fish. He's quite the outdoorsman.

Stetson Troy Boswell, 1st deer, Nov. 2010

We finally got a girl, Channing Rae Boswell, on July 19, 2004. She is a joy! I remember her first haircut by her Aunt Rhonda. It was the first time she called me "Grand Baba". She is all girl but has a lot of spunk. She loves to have her fingernails painted, put on make-up and get dressed-up but she can also hang with the boys. She tries to keep everyone straight! I am continually telling Tondra that Channing is just like her; bossy and looks just like her. It is as though Tondra had spit Channing right out of her mouth.

Channing at Preschool Graduation, 2009

Canyon Jones Boswell was born August 26, 2008, and they say he is the last. Canyon loves his Pop as all of them do. He loves to ride anything that moves: golf-cart, four-wheeler, tractor; it doesn't matter as long as he is moving and with Pop, he is happy. I think God sent Canyon to us to keep us young! He definitely keeps us busy.

Grandchildren are so different from your own children. The girls like to tell people that their kids do some of the same things they used to do, the only difference is we spanked them for doing it and we laugh when our grandkids do them.

Canyon at the beach

Treasured Memories of Our Grandchildren

Wednesday night, April 28, 2004, Levi trusted God as his Savior at Gillsville Baptist Church. He was 10.

December 2009, Gatlin trusted Jesus as his Savior at a youth retreat in Gatlinburg, Tennessee, with his youth pastor Saul McCoy. Gatlin was 13 years old.

June 22, 2006, Devin came to the house and announced that he had gotten saved on Thursday at Gillsville Baptist Church. Rev. Bill Calhoun was the pastor. Devin was 9 years old.

August 4, 2008, Stetson was saved at Gillsville Baptist Church. Rev. Bill Calhoun was the pastor. He was nine years old.

June 22, 2011 Channing finally lost her first tooth-Pop pulled it.

August 26, 2010, Canyon called me "Grandbaba" and gave up his pacifier. He and Channing flushed it down the commode. Rob had the privilege of getting it out of the bathroom pipes. He was two years old.

Canyon, Levi, Gatlin, Stetson, Devin, & Channing

My Life's Sudden Change...

*For we know that if our earthly house of this tabernacle were
dissolved, we have a building of God, and house not made with
hands, eternal in heaven.*

II Corinthians 5:1KJV

My last job was working as a secretary for the Banks County
Extension Service at the Banks County Courthouse. When I began
there in 1980, little did I know of what my future would hold.
November 4, 1997, I went upstairs via the elevator to the 2nd floor
as usual but suddenly my eyes became blurry and all I could see was
a form in front of me. June, one of the office secretaries at the Clerk
of Court, immediately called 911. They took my blood pressure and
it was 110/90. Mr. John Mitchell, my employer, drove me home
that day.

My next strange episode came on November 15, 1997. While I
was at home on the sofa my right arm suddenly felt heavy and I could
not use it. Troy drove me to Northeast Georgia Medical Center in
Gainesville and I was admitted to the hospital. I was paralyzed on
my right side; I could not move my right arm or leg and there was no
feeling on the right side of my body. After eight days and no change,
Dr. James Parks gave orders for a MRI, CAT scan, EKG, and x-ray.
He agreed that it was a light stroke. Eventually, the paralysis went
away and everything was back to normal.

A few weeks after coming home, I went to my neighbor, Betty
Meeks' home one afternoon; with pants for her to hem (she was a
seamstress). While I was sitting in her swing, I started to see double.
When she saw me holding my head, Betty asked "What's wrong with
you"? I told her it would pass but she was very concerned! Betty

asked me if she could drive me home and I told her "No, it will pass in a little while". The very next Sunday at Mt. Carmel, Betty asked me in front of Troy if I told him about seeing double. She told Troy that I needed to be seen by a doctor. She said "That's not something you fool around with".

My second stroke happened about two months later on January 9, 1998. I woke up during the night with the urge to urinate. When I tried to get up, I stumbled. I could not pick up my left foot. I thought it was another episode of vertigo (which I had been experiencing recently). However, I was paralyzed on my left side. Dr. Parks said it was not a stroke but looked like Multiple Sclerosis. I told Dr. Parks that my sister had been diagnosed with MS and was seeing a doctor in Athens; a neurologist named Dr. C. Van Morris.

On January 23, 1998, I finally went to see Dr. Morris. In March, after months of testing, Dr. Morris and the radiologist, Dr. Jerry Smith, both said they were seeing something that they had never seen before. There was something on the left side of the motor area of my brain. They thought it was some kind of lesions but were not completely sure. I was devastated by the news. On March 21, 1998, someone knocked at my back door. It was Carl & Becky Clough, friends of ours from church. I began to cry. I just found out about the lesions on my brain. I shared with them what Dr. Morris had told me. On March 23, 1998, Dr. Morris made me an appointment with Dr. Jane Gilmore at Emory University in Atlanta. We continued to see her for a few months. Finally, she decided to do a brain biopsy to look closer at the lesions. While I was at Emory, I was also tested for MS. The test for MS is extremely painful. Spinal fluid is extracted with a needle through a lumbar puncture. I had this procedure performed nine times! It was so painful that I would grit my teeth together and scream. I finally told the nurses to stop, that my God would handle it! Emory's results were inconclusive and I continued to get worse. I will never leave thee, nor forsake thee. Hebrews 13:5 KJV

Dr. Morris called Duke University in Durham, North Carolina, and talked with Dr. Allen Freidman, a neurologist. I was to go there for another brain biopsy. On the way to Duke, Ruth Justus, our neighbor called the local radio station and had them play *Almighty God* by Michael Combs. As Troy and I heard it on the radio, we began to pray. While I was there, my radiologist, Dr. Smith flew his father, my pastor, Brother Ralph O. Smith, over to see me. Reverend Jeff Morgan and his wife Stacy, the Pastor of Gillsville Baptist Church also came. What a blessing and a surprise! Kathy, Rhonda, and Tondra also drove up for my surgery.

June 17, 1999, while at Duke, I told my grand-boys to keep looking up because God loves you. I told them, "I want to see you saved by God's grace, love and compassion. Children are the hands by which we take hold of heaven."

After only a few days at Duke, I was released, but not ready to travel such a long distance. On the way home we had a strange encounter. I really don't remember much about it but Troy describes it as an encounter with an angel.

We were on the interstate and suddenly I felt sick. I told Troy but we were in the left lane and couldn't stop in time. I threw up everywhere; all over Troy, the car, and me. What a mess! We exited off the interstate and Troy found the closest gas station. I was in no condition to be alone in a bathroom. I could barely sit up in the car; my brain biopsy had only been three days before. The biopsy site was wrapped up on the left side of my head with white gauze to keep out germs. Troy said he had no idea what he was going to do-everyone and everything was a mess.

As soon as the car came to a stop a woman walked up to my door. She opened it and said "I'll take care of her." She took me to the bathroom and helped me change my clothes and get cleaned up while Troy changed clothes and cleaned up the car. When he returned I was in the car and the woman was no where to be found. I don't recall this happening because of my memory during the time I was sick, but our family believes this was an angel sent by God when I desperately needed help.

On June 20, 1999, as I was recuperating at home after my brain biopsy, my friend Brenda Whitfield sent the prettiest dozen red roses. I would wake up and the roses would be right next to me. I began thinking about how each bud stood for something and how we were just like those flowers. They are so beautiful for a little while and then they begin to wither away.

What we do with our life is our choice, whether we serve God or the Devil. Life is a beautiful gift God has given to us. If we trust Jesus Christ as our Savior, we will see him in heaven. This was the lesson I learned on January 1982, when my Daddy died. The song just came to my mind: *Just Trust and Obey.*

I tell you the truth, unless you change and become like little children, you will never enter the kingdom of heaven".
Matthew 8:3 KJV

On June 25, 1999, after almost two weeks of sickness after my biopsy with no answers and lots of questions, I was rushed by Banks County Ambulance to Athens Regional Hospital with excruciating pain in my back and stomach. The pain was so severe that it is impossible to describe. It was in the upper part of my back just under my left arm. I was in the hospital for several days but the pain did not stop. The doctors kept increasing my pain medicine, but to little avail. At one point they told my family they could not increase my morphine dosage anymore and it was still not working.

From this point on I don't have much memory of what happened. My daughters have graciously assisted in providing the details of the next few months of my life:

From Tondra:

Mama was in such pain that it was almost unbearable to watch. She would moan and scream and eventually she was being given so much pain medication that she was not aware of who was with her or what was happening-but it was still very obvious that she was in horrible, horrible pain. They began pumping her stomach and this awful dark "stuff" would emerge into the machine. At this time the doctors still did not know what was causing the pain. I was with my dad one day when they came to get Mama for a CT scan. They told us they would bring her back in about 30 minutes to an hour; but Mama didn't come back. Instead, Dr. Morris and two other doctors finally came to the room. They told us they had found the problem and Mama had a blockage in her small intestines which was causing the pain. They would have to do emergency surgery and did not know if she would survive the surgery. Dr. David Sailors and Dr. Michael West would be performing the surgery with Dr. Morris as soon as the operating room was ready. We were in shock. I quickly called my sister who was at work in Gainesville, nearly an hour away. I told her to come as quick as she could. They had already taken Mama to prep her for surgery and we were not sure if Rhonda would get to see her or not. My Aunt Kathy and my Aunt Carolyn, Mama's sister, came quickly also. Rhonda finally made it and was able to see Mama just before she entered the operating room. The nurses realized what a serious surgery this was going to be and made an exception to let Rhonda in to see Mama.

We waited in Mama's room for a while and were then moved to a small waiting room. It was filled with family and friends. It seemed like the surgery lasted for hours and honestly I can't remember how long we waited but I do remember what happened when the doctor came in. He told us that because of the blockage Mama had lost the majority of her small intestines. She only had about 13 inches left where a normal person has well over 15 feet and that they didn't know if they would be able to reattach the remaining portion; this would require another surgery. But even if they were successful with the reattachment they still only gave her a 15% chance of surviving. If she survived, we were told that she might not have any quality of life. She would live on a feeding tube, waste away to nothing and be skin and bones. These were just a few of the things that they told us. It was just a wait and see game. We were all devastated. Mom's sister had to be taken to the emergency room soon after we heard the news; she had a mild heart attack and had to be hospitalized. I can still remember my cousin Stan praying in the waiting room that night. There were so many questions; many of which were "Why Barbara, she is such a good person". Over the next few days there were so many visitors and so many calls, it was unbelievable. The hospital operator even commented to one caller "That Barbara Jones must be a really special lady".

The next few days were touch and go. I remember the day of the second surgery. Mama was in ICU and we could only go in to see her every two hours. The nurses told my dad they would leave the door open and we could sit with Mama the entire day until the surgery. They didn't say it, but I know they did not expect her to survive and wanted us to have all the time we could with her. The doctors, to their surprise, were able to reattach the intestines. There was a small amount of "living" intestines left that they could attach to. However, their reports were still very grim and they offered little hope. We were told that with conditions like Mama's, patients usually didn't recover. Mama was on a ventilator and we didn't know what the result would be. She had tubes and wires everywhere. My dad stayed by my mom's side day and night. He rarely left the hospital for weeks and weeks. I don't think he slept in his own bed for over a month-and he kept working.

After many days they began to wean Mama off of the ventilator. Weeks went by and we just kept praying. I did not want my Mama to have to live in a vegetative state; I knew she would not want this. Rhonda and I prayed that she would live in a way that she could enjoy life-especially her grandchildren.

It was not an easy battle. One day they could reduce the ventilator and she would be fine but the next day they would have to increase it again; but little by little, slowly she was off. She was awake and eventually she was talking again. It was a miracle! Daddy said, Praise God, he has been there through it all.

As it tells us in the scriptures, "God will never leave us, nor forsake us". During this miraculous time in our lives, God was right there with us every step of the way. Watching this miracle unfold in front of our eyes is why we are sharing this story. It's worth telling again and again.

Dr. Morris was a God fearing man. The doctors honestly didn't expect this but the miracles didn't stop there. The next hurdle was for her intestines to "wake-up". If the reconnection was not successful she would have to wear a colostomy bag. Several times each day the nurses and doctors would listen to her stomach for signs that her intestines were "waking up". I can remember the day that Daddy called with the good news: The nurse had heard it! Her intestines were working-I don't know if I have ever heard such excitement in my Daddy's voice. Once again, it was a miracle!

After about six weeks in the hospital the Doctor's were not sure why she was still alive. Every doctor who saw her told us it was a true miracle. Medically, she should not be alive. Mama continued to improve and after weeks and weeks in the hospital it was finally time for her to come home. She had a port in her left upper chest for a feeding tube that fed straight into her veins. She would have a hospital bed, she was not eating any food, could not care for herself, had to have medication and shots several times daily, she had constant diarrhea, and she would need constant round the clock care. It would be a huge job to take care of mama.

Home Sweet Home....

From Rhonda:

When we arrived home, Mom had a central line surgically placed in the left part of her upper chest. Since she had lost most of her intestines, there was no way for her body to absorb the nutrients from the food and medicine by mouth. Each day she received a large bag of nutrition through IV to survive. She was on blood thinner injections, for blood clots that were still in her intestine and had constant diarrhea. There were more medicines than I could count and she could hardly sit up in the bed. The first evening at home was so stressful to everyone. A home health nurse came to help us set up our "clinic". Who knew my dad and I would receive a whole year of nursing training in only a few hours? Daddy learned to give Mama shots in her stomach while I learned how to change a central surgical dressing. We both learned how to attach IV bags of different medicines and nutrition while trying to keep her comfortable. It was so over whelming; so much for all of us. I remember my dad saying, "I can't stay out of work much longer. Your mother may have to go into a nursing home. For a little while." Just until she did not need twenty-four hour a day care. It seemed our only option. Mama was so upset; she did not want to go into a nursing home, but she also new that Daddy had missed many weeks of work.

One night I talked to Mama and Daddy and told them "I think I'm going to quit my job and take care of Mama". We worked it out so that they paid me some to help with Devin's daycare, and Levi was in kindergarten that year.

Taking care of Mama was a full time job. With only thirteen inches of intestines she could not control her bowels. She could eat and wanted to eat, but whatever she ate would go straight through her and she had to wear diapers.

Daddy and I had a system in place. At night Daddy would give her a shot in her stomach and hook her up to the IV nutrition machine that would run twelve hours. We had it set so that I would have time to get Levi to school, and get back to turn the IV machine off. I would flush the lines, change her diaper, and get her ready for the next day. Everyday we had a routine; take all those medicines, check her blood pressure and temperature and if she got up from the hospital bed I would weigh her. I kept a chart on her, just like the doctor's office did.

Mama complained that the days went by so slowly, but it felt like there was not enough time in the day to get everything done. I would cook lunch and supper, bathe and change her, clean the incisions from surgery, and take care of the central line. Some days were better than others. We found that central lines could become blocked and that would mean having more small surgeries to replace it.

Going to doctor's appointments were tasks in themselves. Mama could barely get into a wheelchair to go to the restroom much less travel 45 minutes to Athens and sit in a waiting room for 30 minutes. Then we would see one of her doctors and travel back home. But somehow we did it many times.

A few months passed and we started to adjust to our situation. Mama began to get her strength back a little at a time. She would sit up in a chair for a little while and started to feed herself. But still our daily routine was full from 8:00 am to 5:00pm.

A Light at the End of the Tunnel....

My memory from this point on is more vivid:

Rhonda knew that when she had to unhook my IV machine each morning, I was going to have a bowel movement within the next 20 to 30 minutes. So when I was able to walk to the bedside toilet, she wanted me to try to get up. But I did not feel the need. I was so tired and just wanted to stay in my bed. Well low and behold, just like she said, I would have accidents. This created more work for her. Now let me tell you, it was wonderful having Rhonda taking care of me. But some days, we would get so aggravated with each other. We could hardly stand to be in the same room. We always began a new day with a new attitude.

We learned what foods I should eat and which ones to stay away from. Usually if I stayed away from greasy foods my stomach was better because I had no control over my bowels. When I would get the urge to use the restroom, it was usually too late. Eventually, I started getting up like Rhonda wanted. Later on I gained better control of my bowels. But boy did I still have accidents.

If there is one thing I love besides Troy and my family; it is food! Each time Rhonda would take me to the doctor I would want to stop by a fast food restaurant and get something to eat. Rhonda would always want me to wait until I got home, or to get something like grilled chicken so it would not be so hard on my stomach, but I didn't want grilled chicken. I wanted a Big Mac or a Whopper and I wanted to eat it as soon as I got it, not when I got home like Rhonda wanted me to do. Well some days I would barely make it home and some days I wouldn't, and those days were bad.

One day while Rhonda was weighing me something interesting happened: I had gained a pound! On my next trip to the doctor Rhonda brought my weight chart with us. She wanted to discuss my weight gain with my doctor. Rhonda showed him the chart and he, too, was puzzled. Rhonda wondered if maybe I was getting nutrition from the IV *and* the food I was eating. Dr. Morris agreed and suggested that I only use the IV every other night.

Well, I continued to gain weight. Dr. Morris took me off my IV every two nights and eventually another miracle happened: my weight continually increased and I came off IV nutrition all-together. One doctor told us he had never used the word miracle before, because he didn't believe in miracles, but this was a true miracle. You see the doctors had told me I would never gain weight without IV nutrition because I was not able to extract nutrients.

Dr. Morris still wanted me to keep my central line for a little while just in case I needed nutrition again. But it never happened. Praise God! I remember having my last surgery to have my central line removed. What a great day it was! I felt free as a bird. Praise God! I did not have to worry about the port coming out of my chest. I could turn over in my bed if I wanted too.

I remember the day I finally got up out of my bed to take a bath. That was another great day that God had given me. I just couldn't stop praising God, my Savior for everything He had done for me. Each day was getting a little easier. Rhonda did not have to do everything for me, and that felt good too. As time moved on, I began doing a few things for myself.

One morning as Rhonda was reading the newspaper and she noticed an ad for a preschool teacher from 8:00 am until noon at Homer Baptist Church. Rhonda said that would be perfect for her. She could do that in the mornings and still take me to doctor's appointments in Athens in the afternoons and help me cook. Rhonda applied for the position and got it! She began teaching a three-year-old class three days a week and is now the Preschool Director. Little is much when God is in it.

This was good for me because I had to depend on myself more. I was getting out working in my flower garden and even beginning to cut a little grass. Since my sickness I have learned to drive the golf cart and get around well. We all live close together so I can drive the golf cart to visit my grandchildren. Slowly, I began to cook again and now I cook like I did before. I realized that I would never be as I once was, but God wanted me on this earth for a purpose.

Finally, after looking at the results from testing at Duke, Dr. Morris had a diagnosis: Homocystilitis. My levels of B-12, B-6, and Folic Acid were too high and that can cause strokes and an aneurysm. Dr. Morris wanted my girls to have their levels checked as well. Tondra's levels were good but Rhonda's levels were the same as mine. Our levels are routinely checked and Rhonda has to take one Folic Acid pill a day and I have to take two pills a day for the rest of my life but all is good. Little is much when God is in it!

Below are commentaries from friends about this trying time:

From Reverend Ralph O. Smith

My name is Rev. Ralph O. Smith, former pastor of Mt. Carmel Baptist Church in Banks County, Georgia. During the time that I was pastor there, Troy and Barbara Jones attended church at Mt. Carmel and I counted it an honor to be their pastor. Barbara in 1997 became very sick. I will let her tell you about her illness.

What I want to tell you about is how they reacted to her illness as Christians. I never heard Troy or Barbara ask God "Why, God?" I believe they were trusting as in the following scripture.

And we know that all things work together for good to them that love God, to them who are the called according to his purpose.

Romans 8:28 KJV

God is our refuge and strength, a very present help in trouble. Psalm 46:1 KJV

Barbara was in the hospital for over a month at Athens Regional Hospital. When I visited her, she was always glad to see me. She was never discouraged knowing that she was in the hands of the all-powerful God.

One morning I got out of bed and thought I needed to go see Barbara so I called my son, Dr. Jerry O. Smith, he offered his plane when I told him what I wanted to do. He told me to come on down to Athens, Georgia and we flew to Duke University Hospital in North Carolina. When we got there, we found a family that was trusting God.

I will lift up mine eyes unto the hills, from whence cometh my help. My help cometh from the Lord, which made heaven and earth. Psalm 121:1,2 KJV

I thank God for doctors and nurses and their care and compassion. After the medical personnel have performed surgery and given all their medical care, God is the only one who can heal.

I thank God for what he has done for the Jones family. My wife and I have many fond memories of our 30 years and 5 months we were allowed to pastor Mt. Carmel Baptist Church. We are glad Troy and Barbara and our families have crossed paths in this life. May God Bless you are our prayer.

Reverend Ralph O. Smith

Rev. Ralph and Ruby Smith Pastor Mt. Carmel Baptist Church 1969-2000"

From Sarah Carlan:

Barbara,

You and I have been friends for many, many years. Our kids grew up together in school and church. Our most memorable times, I suppose, are the many vacations that we have shared. We have been many places, especially the beach that have blessed us with unforgettable memories. We laughed and we cried as we have shared experiences that will last us a lifetime. Remember the time that you had to return home in the middle of the night during a wild and scary thunderstorm. The time we had to visit the dentist or the time we had to shop to clean up a mess someone left in the house .We were to stay at before, we would even consider putting our luggage inside. The good times far out measured the bad. All the shopping we have shared. I can't imagine the money we spent but oh how we enjoyed those trips. On many occasions, all the girls went to Panama City, St. Simons and various other places. What a great time we have shared through the years. On those trips we talked about our families, our children, our lives and how God had blessed us.

I remember the day vividly when I was told that you were so critically ill. My brother, his wife, and their son Cody, Paul and myself had vacationed in New York State. As we were returning, (coming across the Georgia, South Carolina border) my family told me that they had received a phone call from someone telling that you were so sick that the outcome wasn't looking very good. I cried and was so upset the rest of the way home. It was late in the night when we arrived home, therefore, I waited until morning to go to Athens Regional Hospital. There were lots of people in the waiting room as you were going in for surgery that morning. I don't remember who they were, except Joan Cochran. We stood in the doorway. I cried and cried after Dr. West came and told us that you might not return from surgery. Thank God you did come out of the surgery and was placed in ICU. I can't remember how long it was before getting to see you. John Mitchell and I went back together to see you. I held your hand and talked to you but you were unable to respond. Later on when you had recovered enough to be brought out of intensive care, I was able to come and stay with you while Troy and the girls got some sleep.

You were able to sit up while the nurses changed your bed. You could speak some but you were still unable to take care of your basic needs. I was privileged to help you then, as I will always be there if you need me, ever. What a blessing when you were able to return home. God had more blessings for you, and you had more to give to others.

I am going to close by saying this and by sharing this poem that you wrote for me many, many years ago. Barbara, we have traveled life's journey together here and I know by our faith in God that when our journey ends on this earth that our true journey will have just begun.

Here we go, there we go
Where we end up, nobody ever knows!
A FRIEND by far, you'll always be
Let's hit the mall, just you and me!
Gain a pound, lose a pound
Swap those books all around!
Exercise you plainly see
Has been working for you and me!
A FRIEND FOREVER I'll always be
Remember Barbara you can count on me!

Friend Forever,
Sarah Carlan

From Becky Clough

It was a Wednesday night, church night. Carl and I had a discussion as to whether or not we would go to church or go to Athens Regional Hospital. We decided that we needed to go to the hospital to be supportive of Barbara Jones' family. At the time, we didn't think that Barbara would live. We had no idea that we would be able to see her either. When we arrived at the hospital, we went to the waiting room. There were a number of people there including our pastor Ralph Smith and his son, Dr. Jerry Smith. Barbara's daughter, Rhonda, motioned for us to come with her. She told us that we would be able to see Barbara because she was going to take us back there. I will never forget what we saw. There was Barbara just lying there so still.

We could not believe it! After standing back there with Rhonda and talking to her for a while, we went back to the waiting room. Barbara's brother asked someone who we were. Then he came over to talk with us. When we were young children, Barbara and her parents lived in the house just below ours for a short time. Occasionally Barbara would come up to the house and stay for a short period of time. We sat there and talked for awhile catching up on things. When we got up to leave, Barbara's brother, his wife and Dr. Jerry Smith walked out with us. We stood in the lobby and talked for awhile longer. I will never forget Dr. Jerry's words; "People who are in the condition that Barbara is in never leave the hospital alive". After Dr. Jerry left, we continued to talk with Barbara's brother for a long time. I knew that the Lord could touch Barbara and heal her. My Dad spent six weeks in the hospital due to a chain saw accident. When he rewired the chain saw, it kicked back causing the handle to knock a hole in his intestines. He was at the point of death three times. The last time he had surgery, we were so afraid that we would lose him. It was looking doubtful that he would come out of the hospital alive. My youngest daughter's teacher stopped her class one morning to pray for him. I know that the Lord heard her prayer and many others that went up that day. About the same time of day that she was praying, my Dad took a turn for the better. He is still alive today at a ripe old age of 86. From this firsthand experience, I knew in my heart that God could touch Barbara. In my mind, I can still see the vision of her at the hospital. I can hear the words of Dr. Jerry Smith, but the evidence of God's work is before us today. God is so real!

MY PRAYER WARRIORS...

During my illness, the hundreds of cards were wonderful and so up-lifting and inspiring. As Rev. Ralph would say me, Keep Looking Up. I felt compelled, "That's why I wrote this manuscript." I was lead by the Holy Spirit. Everyone had such and impact in lifting me up, I decided to send all the card fronts to St. Judes Children Hospital where they would restore and make new cards to raise money for the children and lift up others as well.

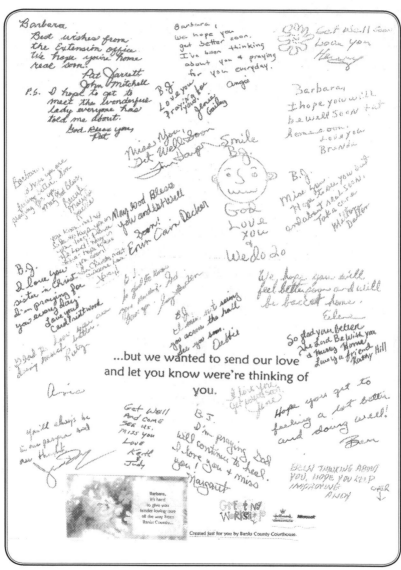

Get Well Wishes from Banks County Courthouse employees,
Homer, GA. My friends all called me "B.J."

Laverne sends a Happy Birthday wish in 1998

Bookmarks made for Grand-Baba by Levi, Devin, Gatlin, Stetson, 2004

Get Well Wishes

We're lifting you to GOD in prayer,

Asking HIM to extend to you HIS love,

May HIS healing touch be comforting to you, and

May HIS reassuring voice bring you hope and strength.

From

Chattahoochee Baptist Church
Adult Sunday School Class

Wait on the Lord;
be of good courage,
and He shall strengthen
thine heart.

Psalm 27:14

You are in our Prayers!

May God
be very close to you
and in His special way
Restore your health,
renew your strength,
and bless you day by day.

Hoping You'll
Soon Be Well!

Adult Sunday School Class
Chattahoochee Baptist Church

[signatures]

**Get Will Wish from Chattahoochee Baptist Church Adult
Sunday School Class**

"God Bless You Picture" from Carol, Margaret, Erlene, Erin, Debbie, Brenda, June, Jenie and Nancy

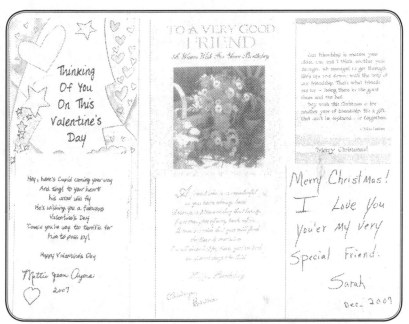

**Happy Valentines Day-Mattie Jean Ayers,
Get Well Wish-Bertha Roberts
Merry Christmas-Sarah Carlan**

all 3 of these card's were received in 2007

Levi penciled this out for Grand-Baba

The Good, The Bad and The Ugly.....

It was brought to my attention that when you're writing a book about life, you can't leave out the ugly. It's easy to write about the good and bad, but the ugly is a whole different story. What is the ugly you ask? Well, the ugly is the sin in your life that keeps you from being closer to God, your family and your friends. The ugly is never seen at work or church and your friends have probably never seen it as well. It never leaves your home but is with you every second of the day.

I guess by now you are very curious about my ugly. My ugly has been haunting me most all of my adult life. It has brought me happiness and joy for brief moments in my life, but for the most part it has destroyed a piece of the love that Troy and I have shared over the years. There are not many people who truly know about my ugly, but now I am going to share it with you.

When I was growing up my mother made sure we had everything I needed and most everything I wanted. So when I got married and had children, I wanted the same. Troy was very conservative and wanted to save money and I liked to buy things. Troy always said "Only buy things you have the money to pay for". His idea of buying a new outfit was going to Sky City and mine was going to Mary's Fashion Shoppe for something special for me or my girls.

This is where my ugly began. I would buy things that cost a lot and tell Troy that I paid much less for them. I wanted birthdays and Christmas to be out of this world. Troy would ask how much I spent and I would say, "Oh, not that much. I've been saving and buying all year long". Troy did not believe in credit cards and he did not have a clue how many I had.

You see, I had really good credit. I made my minimum payments each month and on time. My only problem was making sure that

Troy never went to the mailbox. I had to make sure that I always got there first. My problem was not only making Christmas and birthdays great - I was a compulsive buyer. If I saw it and wanted it, I would buy it. If I wanted to remodel my house, I would do it and pay for it later. For years I carried around an Electrolux vacuum cleaner in the trunk of my car because it cost so much and Troy would have killed me (not literally) if he had known. I would use it and then put it back in the car. He had no idea how much debt I had accumulated. At times I wanted to tell him, but I was afraid he would leave me.

I carried this burden with me, but I still could not stop. I would wake up in the night and wonder how I was going to pay all this money back. I would try to think of people that might loan me this kind of money. Not only did I have credit card bills, but I also had a bank note with nothing really to show.

I finally got my bank note paid off but instead of putting that money on my credit cards and other bills I owed, I decided to buy a new car. I remember Rhonda telling me I was crazy. But I just had to have it - I could not help myself. I bought a 1997 Chevrolet Malibu. It was beige in color and when I bought it, I loved the car. The only problem was I hated the color beige. Why would I buy a beige car? Then my car payments began and I was living paycheck to paycheck, all the while living a lie. I was in over my head and could not tell anyone. You have heard of the old saying *"Borrowing from Peter to pay Paul"*? This is what I was doing. My girls knew a little about my money problems and if I did not get home in time to get the mail before Troy, I had given them the job of doing so.

In a moment my life changed - I had my first stroke. I did not realize until later that God wanted me to come clean about my sin. I just worried about how I was going to pay all this money back without anyone finding out. You see this was not $5,000 or even $10,000. This was close to $30,000 of debt. By this time my girls had gotten older and had families of their own. One day I was talking to Rhonda about the money I owed and she told me about a loan officer in Commerce who could consolidate all my credit cards and bills with a lower interest rate so that I would not pay out so much money each month.

My second stroke came and I was never the same. That's when my life really changed. I was no longer able to go to the bank, I could not work, and most of all I could not go to the mailbox. Troy eventually figured out my ugly. I cannot imagine how he felt. My life to him was a lie. He had been saving for retirement all his life and I had been spending all my life. How could he ever forgive me? We worked through things and eventually I received my disability and early retirement from the University of Georgia. This was enough to make my payments, pay for my medicine, and make it through the month.

This was after I talked with Rhonda, she arranged for me to pay $400.00 a month for four years. It was deducted from my checking account. The bank would automatically pay it. I did finally pay that note off. Troy finished paying for my car and then later sold it. What a great time in my life when my note was paid, my car was gone and no more payments. The only demand from Troy was to cut up my credit cards and never have them again. So that's just what I did, the cards are gone.

Troy and I have always kept our money separate. He would give money to pay all the utilities bills, insurance, etc., but we could never see eye to eye on money. He was stingy and wanted to save and I wanted to buy things. In the end I guess it was good that he was that way, if not he would probably have to work for the rest of his life if our money was together.

For a while I did well because I could not go out and see things I wanted. I was basically confined to the house, only leaving to go to the doctor which wore me out. One day while Troy was working and I was at home alone watching TV, I came across the Home Shopper's Network. And it happened - I fell in love. I would find myself watching all day. Everything on those channels was wonderful, beautiful things I just had to have. I began to order lots of things. However, I paid for everything before ordering it. Troy had the channels blocked so we could not get these televisions stations,

Now days I am doing a lot better with my ugly. I have it under control somewhat, but it still pops up from time to time. I struggle with the little voice inside me that's suppose to say, "Barbara you don't need that," instead I hear: "Oh yes, you do, you have to have it". Whether its food, clothes, jewelry or whatever, I just have to have it. Not only for myself, but other people. If I see something that I know someone would love, I often buy it for them.

In October of 2003, I was debt free, PRAISE GOD--it's just like Brother Martin Luther King, Jr. said "Free at last". Free to look at something, think how beautiful it is and walk away, free to know there is money in my account to pay for my medicine, and most of all, the freedom of Troy to trust me. Pray for my ugly, that I will one day have it under complete control. That I will tell the old devil to get behind me, because God is the one in whom I trust. PRAISE GOD MY SAVIOR.

May God bless you and your loved ones. I pray that if there is an ugly in your life, whatever it may be, and the secret that only you and God know, it will be recognized and changed at this very moment in your life.

Today My Life...

It has now been 12 years since my surgery and to the doctor's amazement I am living vibrantly! and I still have bowel accidents, it happens often. I will remain this way until I die. It is very important that I have a rest room nearby. **BUT I CAN ALWAYS LOOK AROUND** and see someone worse off than me. I am **sooooo very BLESSED!** I took early retirement and I spend my time praising my Lord and thanking God for my grandchildren. I have enjoyed spending many wonderful days at the Banks County Senior Center. I wasn't used to being cooped up inside, not being able to go when I wanted. Since my strokes and sickness, I don't drive anymore, so I look forward to trips and outings with my friends at the Senior Center. I look forward to seeing all my friends and playing Skip-Bo, a card game. It's a home away from home!!!

2010 The Crew from The Center

Troy & Beatrice Simmons at Savannah Beach 2006

Savannah Beach 2006 What a great trip!

I take many medications and have to go to the doctor every two weeks or monthly to keep a check on my blood, it must be maintain between 2 or 3 either thick or thin. I no longer eat any green leafy vegetables, broccoli, spinach, cauliflower, Brussels sprouts, or cabbage. Otherwise, I do not have a feeding tube and can eat anything I want. I never "wasted away to nothing". Instead I am proud to say I weigh 156 pounds. Praise to my God.

In October 2008, Troy retired from Scovill Manufacturing Company, Clarksville, GA. During this time we have done some traveling. We have visited the Amish Country, Grand Canyon, and Niagara Falls. We are very active in our church; I sing in the choir and Troy is a deacon. We have many Christian friends and enjoy spending time with them. A few years ago Troy became interested in antique cars he now has an A-Model and a T-Model. I remember when he began the restoration of his 1930 A-Model. He brought a 1930 A-Ford chasse and asked Billy, one of his friends, if he would help with the restoration. He ordered the materials to build the car and it arrived as a pile of bolts, nuts, the top, bumpers, and doors. A big *Thank You* goes out to Billy for all those hours spent. We've had some good times in that old car.

**Troy & B.J., William & Carolyn Carpenter,
Billy & Mary Sue Meeks**

Life is like a highway you only travel down once, thank God.

But seek you first the kingdom of God, and his righteousness; and all these things shall be added unto you.
            Matthew 6:33 KJV

Troy and I often take short trips with friends that are also Model-A owners. Jack and Pat own a 1928 A-Model Ford and Joe and Carolyn own a 1929 A-model Ford. Carolyn is a scrap booker and takes pictures of every trip. She also keeps a diary of where we eat, where we spent the night, and what we did. We have had great times and it is a wonderful blessing of God.

Barbara & Troy 1930 Ford Model A

Pat & Jack 1928 Model A

Carolyn & Joe 1929 Model A

There is another group of friends that get together throughout the year: some of them attend church with us and some are lifelong friends: Carl and Becky, Dave and Sandra, Paul and Sarah, and Billy and Brenda and Elaine. And of course, Larry, he's the clown of this group. We've been getting together for about 30 years. When you get Troy, Carl, Dave, Larry, Billy and Paul together you had better be on your toes.

In 2007, Laverne, Larry's wife went home to meet Jesus our Savior. We shared some wonderful times together before the Lord Jesus Christ called her home.

2010 Annual New Year's Eve Gathering

Troy and I are more active in our church than we have ever been. We want to serve God who has been so good to us. I would like to share some of what we are doing in our church and community.

On February 6, 2011, I was sitting in church; a woman named Jo Davis was sitting in front of me. We both noticed that a young girl named Taylor Cash appeared to be under conviction from God. A woman sitting next to her, Mrs. Davis, looked at her and asked if she had ever been saved. Taylor looked up toward her father with questions in her eyes? He said, this is one decision you have to make on your own. Just follow your heart! Taylor reached out to me and those arms went straight around my neck. We made our way to the altar and I asked Brother Daryl to pray with us and Mr. Davis. We all prayed and Taylor asked Jesus to come into her heart. She was 12 years old. When Taylor asked to be baptized her father did also.

On another Sunday in February, Troy was involved in a playground planning meeting and we had just finished lunch at church when Brother Bobby suggested that we take a plate to a gentleman that lived across the road from the church. He was a shut-in and didn't get out much. His name was Henry and he's 86 years old. We fixed the plate and I went with him to take it. I had no idea what God's plan was but I felt he wanted to use me. We knocked on the door and he opened it. He thanked us for the plate of food and we all sat down. We began talking about when he had built his house. He told us that he chose the exact spot so that his mother would be able to walk to church. We continued to talk about his mother and I asked him if he would like to see her again. He said yes, so I shared with him Romans 10:9. I read that verse to him from his own Bible. That if you will confess Jesus with your mouth and believe in your heart that God raised Jesus from the dead then you will be saved.

I explained to him that he could substitute his name and then he took the Bible and read it for himself. He read, if Henry will confess with his mouth the Lord Jesus, and shall believe in thy heart that God hath raised him from the dead then Henry shall be saved.

Brother Henry looked up at us and said, "I believe this!"

I was praising God and thanking God for saving Brother Henry! That was old but beautiful floral carpet that we were bowing our knees on. With what I felt in my heart I knew that the Father, Christ Jesus, and the Holy Spirit was with us also; I'm looking forward to seeing Brother Henry and his mama Sister Icie Mize in heaven some day. Praise God.

Henry now goes to lunch on Fridays with Troy, Ted (another neighbor that is confined to home) and Reggie. Reggie lives just a few doors down from us. He is 29 years old and has Freiedrich Ataxia disease. He is confined to a wheelchair or today they would call it a motor operated Roundabout chair. He struggles to breathe at times and has a constant IV. He frequently has to be hospitalized. He is a devoted Christian and he is fighting with godliness.

**Troy & Barbara with Reggie,
our special neighbor and friend"**

When Reggie is able he comes to church on Wednesday nights and Sundays. He also attends Sunday School when he can. Troy and I now attend separate classes. I attend the Ladies class and my teacher is Donna Brown. Troy and Reggie go to the men's class. Earl Nix is the teacher. Reggie struggles daily but God has a plan. Everyone loves Reggie! Reggie is a blessing to everyone. On Mother's day he had his mother drove him to our house to bring an Orchid. It was beautiful! My heart melted; he is still thinking of others!

On November 7, 2010, Reggie was baptized by our pastor, Brother James Duncan.

**Baptism of Reggie, November 7, 2010,
Rev. James Duncan, Mt. Carmel Baptist Church**

I want Jesus to use us, as long as I have breath.
In you I find **PEACE**
In you I find **STRENGTH**
In you **I LIVE** and **MOVE** and **BREATHE**
Everything I say and do is found in **YOU**, my **GOD**
I lift up **Holy Hands**, and let **His Praises Ring**.

Troy and I have a different attitude toward life than we had twelve years ago. I've shared these memories because of my Lord Jesus Christ. God preformed a miracle on my body. I need to share it with others; what God has done for me. Jesus has taught us and has been there with us. I know this because I have experienced his love, peace, healing and understanding in my heart and in my life. I want to love others as though it is the last day to spend on this Earth. My husband and I have dedicated out lives to serving God and to serve him more intensely.

It has been an absolute privilege to share this book with you. I would love to hear from you with anything you would like to share with me. Please email me at littleismuch@yahoo.com.

There are so many memories of friends and family that have meant so much in my life that I wanted to be a part of my book. In memory of my dearest family and friends:

Time has made a change
Since my childhood days
Many of my friend's have gone away
Some I never more in this life see
Time has made a change in me.

In my childhood days I was well and strong
I could climb the hillside all day long
I am not today what I use to be
Time has made a change in me.

**Nancy Camilla Brown Massey
1889-1975
Lonzo Herbert Massey 1883-1957**

Martha Lewallen Poole
October 19, 1882- October 5, 1971
John Harrison Poole
December 26, 1867- February 6, 1867

William Fletcher Poole
August 17, 1913- February 24, 1982

Ida Mae Massey Poole
August 13, 1918-November 4, 1999

Eugene Graftin Poole
October 2, 1938-October 31, 2001

William Horace Jones
April 21, 1927-May 4, 1987
Rosa Belle Westmoreland Jones
October 26, 1927-November 1, 2003

Jerry Wayne Jones
January 16, 1949-July 25, 1996

Lois Estelle Forrester Westmoreland
May 4, 1914-March 4, 2008

Bobby Ray Westmoreland
September 22, 1936-October 20, 2004

Bertha Ward Roberts
January 4, 1937-January 23, 2010

Rev. Shane Wilson
August 10, 1959-June 23, 2009

Marsha Laverne Whitlock Butler
August 28, 1943-May 27, 2006

Stanley Wayne Crocker
August 16, 1946-December 8, 2007

William Henry Galloway
February 26, 1968-August 22, 2009

Janet Marie Johnson Galloway
July 12, 1959-February 24, 2010

Joyce Ray Boswell
July 20, 1941-March 12, 2006

Jimmie Adelle Pritchett Ray
September 26, 1920-September 21, 2010

To others that are still with me who mean so much:

For My Grandchildren

**My Pride & Joy, Gatlin, Grand-Baba, Devin, Pop, Stetson,
Levi, and Baby Channing Rae**

To my grandchildren: Levi, Gatlin, Devin, Stetson, Channing, and Canyon. Upon the death of my Grandmother, a Bible was left to me with God's wishes from my mother, Ida Massey Poole. This verse is from my Grandmother for all my children and grandchildren to learn and remember!

The days of our years are threescore years and ten; and if by reason of strength they were fourscore years, yet is their strength labor and sorrow; for it is soon cut off, and we fly away. Psalms 90:10 KJV

You will always be in the prayers of your GrandBaba Jones. Always keep your priorities in order and work for God's glory. My prayer is that your foundation will always be upon the rock and that rock is Jesus Christ.

Why Do We Marry was written by my coworker Imogene Watts Rylee for her son and it is a promise from God. I, Grand Baba Jones, dedicate this section to my beloved grandchildren and also Imogene's grandchildren and to those that come later.

When you become a responsible adult, Jesus wants each of you to take your wedding vows seriously. Read this with the man or woman that you are about to choose as your soul mate. Take your vows before God and let Him be in complete control. I have seen so many build their marriages on the sand and this will not work. You will have little spats, but turn them over to Jesus. If you do this, GrandBaba Jones promises you, you'll never be sorry. This is not just for my grand children but it's for every person that takes these vows and commitments to each other. God bless and keep each of you!

Why Do We Marry?

The primary reason we marry is because we feel we can achieve greater happiness by being married than by remaining single. The thing we want most from marriage, of course, is love—a love, which is strong, a love, which is deep, a love that is enduring. This kind of love is more difficult to achieve than most of us think. There are three types of love. FIRST, there is romantic love; SECOND, there is friendship love; THIRD, there is self-giving love. Each one of these LOVES has a different effect on our marriage.

The type we are most familiar with is romantic LOVE. Anyone can have this type of love. It's very fragile—here today and gone tomorrow. This type of love is not based on character, commitment and enduring values.

The most serious problem with romantic love is it's usually based more on fantasy than fact. God created us sexual creatures; we have an enormous need for sexual fulfillment. But if romantic love is the only type of love we have sooner or later our marriage will run out of gas. It's quite natural for marriage to begin with romantic love. Only to the extent that love deepens and grows will the union be successful.

Friendship LOVE is even more important than romantic love. Friendship love doesn't come naturally. It has to be cultivated through a lifetime of caring and sharing. One doesn't get close to another person in this way unless he genuinely cares about what's going on in that person's life.

Friendship love comes only to those who care enough about their marriage to work at it—to do things to enrich their relationship. This can be done by SITTING IN THE SWING, LISTENING TO MUSIC, READING TOGETHER, EATING TOGETHER, OR WHATEVER MAKES US HAPPY!

Friendship love springs from the deep respect and appreciation two people have for each other. It involves an intense awareness of each other's needs, longings and dreams. This type of love springs from character and unselfishness. To develop intimacy with each other, we must spend time together sharing joys and sorrows, our hopes and our dreams.

The THIRD type of LOVE which every marriage needs is self-giving love. This is the type of love God has in mind when he said husbands should love their wives as Christ loved the Church. This type of love, loves on when it would be easier to walk away. It's a love that only death can terminate. It's love that can handle deep trials because it's anchored in His will.

Because love in its purest form is lodged in HIs will, God doesn't have to blush when he enjoins men to love their wives as Christ loved the Church and gave himself for it. It's entirely within their power to do so. Christ loved the Church because he chose to love it. There wasn't anything romantic about it. And because he chose to love it, he gave himself for it. He submitted himself to scourging and cruel mocking; he allowed sinful men to nail him to a cross and hang him up to die. He did it because he loved. This is the way God enjoins us to love our mates.

Self-giving LOVE is the purest form of love there is. It can be very costly because it concerns itself with giving more than receiving. It involves one person placing the welfare of another before his own. This type of love is deep. It doesn't fluctuate from hot to cold, as romantic love does, because it's anchored in the will.

Only if we develop all three types of love—ROMANTIC, FRIENDSHIP, AND SELF-GIVING, will our marriages be what

God intends. Only to the extent that all three of these are present in our marriage will the full potential for blessing be reached.

Happy Home Recipe

4 c. of love	5 spoons of hope
2 c. of loyalty	2 spoons of tenderness
3 c. of forgiveness	4 qt. Of faith
1 c. of friendship	1 barrel of laughter

Take love and loyalty; mix it thoroughly with faith. Blend it with tenderness, kindness and understanding; add friendship and hope. Sprinkle abundantly with laughter. Bake it with sunshine. Serve daily with generous helpings.

The Seekers Sunday School Class

God blesses the Seeker's Sunday school Class of which Troy and I are members. Our class elected the Rev. William Shane Wilson as the teacher and Brother Doyle Hulsey was elected to teach every other Sunday. Our class is always ready and willing to help with any need that arises.

On Tuesday, June 23, 2009, due to an extended illness, our teacher Brother Shane passed away. Our church was very saddened at his passing but was comforted by the fact that he was not suffering any longer but most importantly of all, he was with the one whom he loved the most, Jesus. Before his passing, he shared a vision that he had with Hoyt Parks and Carl Clough. That vision was for Mt. Carmel to fund the building of another church in Honduras. He did not want this revealed until July. Brother Carl revealed Shane's vision to the church in July just as Shane had requested. After several months of collecting money, Mr. Parks has been given the money and has already taken it to Honduras. Our church is so proud to be a part of the building of two churches in Honduras.

I wish to dedicate the following poem to William and Ciella Wilson, Shane's parents. Shane's mother found this poem at Shane's home the week after his funeral.

Don't Grieve for Me

When I've been to my last service,
And fade softly on the air
The notes of the last song for me,
And then the final prayer;
When friends arise and slowly walk
Down the long church aisle
For that last look at my cold corpse
As they pass in single file,
There may be words of lottery,
And some may even sneer:
Some may sob, and some may cry,
And some not shed a tear.
But be what may, this much I know:
I will no longer care;
No earthly voice can reach my earthly
As I climb that "Golden Stair."
Now, pen in hand, I am writing to you--
This last request;
Don't grieve for me; don't wish me back,
For I am one most blessed.
I have a hope beyond the grave;
I am secure in God's great love.
I leave this world with all its cares
For a mansion up above.
Though it be hard, please wear a smile;
Rejoice, and praise our God!
"Tis only this old shell of mine
You place beneath the sod.
--Author unknown
In memory of Rev. Shane Wilson

I have a copy of a thank you note sent to our Seeker's class by an older couple in our church. Mrs. Jurelle and Mr. Hugh Smelley are in their nineties and are such a blessing to everyone around them. I would like to share this note:

Dear Shane, Doyle and All the Seekers,

I know I'm late to say "Thank You" for the Christmas gift, but I most certainly haven't forgotten the thoughtful attitude you have for us (the seniors). It surely makes senior years much easier to handle knowing someone cares enough to share their love, kindness and good deeds with someone who has almost run the race. I have really enjoyed my 88 years but I can look back and say I'm sorry I "don't get caught in the web" going through life without him is empty. I tried it, without him for a while, but I found life is worthless without Jesus. Don't try it, you cannot find peace, happiness and contentment without him. He means more than fame, fortune, silver or gold. I have not made my life count like I wish I had, but I'm so glad I accepted him in early years, and coming to church has been one of my great pleasures. So what time I have left, I would like to spend all I'm able in the House of the Lord. I thank him so much for what he has done for me and most certainly I thank the Seekers for in this day and hour, it's good to know we have a younger group of Christians coming on who is interested in God's Word. I really admire young people who take a stand for the Lord. Pray for the church, that it will be more productive and people will come from far and near to hear God's work and worship him. Keep up the good work and let the good times roll.

Love you allowed,
Jurrelle and Hugh Smelley

Women's Missionary Union

One day our Women's Missionary Union had been visiting the Banks and Jackson County nursing home. We were all to meet at Cracker Barrel Restaurant. Donna Brown, our WMU Director, asked for volunteers to give their testimonies at our next meeting. Lisa McClure said she would give her testimony if I would. I asked our pastor, Rev. James Duncan and his wife if they would pray for me so that the Lord would speak through me.

At the next meeting, Becky Clough led the program speaking on faith. She told the WMU about a man getting locked up in a freezer. When they found him the next morning, he was dead. Because they were not sure what had killed him, an autopsy was performed on him. The autopsy showed that he froze to death. However; the freezer was not working and the temperature in the freezer was 61 degrees at the time of his death. The Bible tells us in Luke 12:28 "Oh ye of little faith." If only we had the faith of a mustard seed.

At the meeting Lisa McClure, Ciella Wilson, Betty Meeks and I, with the Lord's help, gave our testimonies. I was so excited about my testimony that I told Brother James and Sister Sandra that together, the Lord and I successfully gave my testimony. This was the first time I had shared about my sickness and my miracles and I knew that I needed to continue to tell others.

I received this Wonderful card that delighted my soul in the mail and it said:

Dear Barbara,
Praise the Lord! What a blessing to hear the wonderful ways that God has blessed you. Thank you for sharing your testimony with us. God loosened your tongue and blessed our hearts!

Love,
Sandra Duncan

Hebrews 13:15-16 KJV
By him therefore let us offer up our sacrifices of praise to God continually, that is, the fruit of our lips giving thanks to his name.16 but to do good and to communicate forget not: for with such "sacrifices God is well pleased.

Rev. James and Sandra Duncan, Pastor Mt. Carmel Baptist Church, 2000-Present*

Our Church

On a Sunday during revival at Mt. Carmel in November, 2009, I was praising God for all the wonderful things that He had done for me. Revival was being led by Rev. Doyle Conley, the Pastor of B.C. Grant Baptist Church in Alto. Our choir director, Darrell Davis was singing *I'm Trusting you Lord*. The Holy Spirit came over Bro Darrell. He began to cry and talk all at the same time. He was praising God. I felt the Holy Spirit that night; it was the best feeling! Words can't even describe it. When the choir was through singing, Bro. Darrell asked for everyone to have a time of fellowship and shaking hands with one another. I went to Rev. Conley to shake hands. He told me that my spirit had shaken hands with his spirit and that we were on our way to heaven. Each one of us decided, according to the judgment we feel ourselves to be Christ like.

I came home and worked some more on my book. I read Matthew chapters 6 & 7.

Matt. 6:33 says, But seek ye first the Kingdom of God and his righteous; and all these things shall be added unto you. I read this verse over and over until I had memorized it. I was so excited. I could not wait for 7:00 to come. I went back and shared with Bro. Conley what God had done for me! It was a great revival. I had God in my heart and that was all that mattered.

Jesus, help me keep my eyes on you. Remind me not to worry about what others are doing. Please keep me focused on you.

I am so encouraged by many church friends who tell me that I am a blessing to them, it inspires me. Often they tell me that they watch me singing in the choir and God blesses them just watching me. When I raise my hand in praise to my God, it's from the words I am singing. I am not a great singer, so it is not my voice that brings the blessing. There is a line in the great old hymn *How Great Thou Art* that describes how I feel.

It is the part that says, "Then sings my soul, my Savior God to thee..." That's me!

Time and sickness may have stifled my natural voice and may have caused my words to be slow and faltering, but the song rises high to the Lord above. He understands exactly every word I try to speak! He understands the cry of my heart and the praise that I so long to give to him. It is my praise, to Him and to Him alone, that others see.

God has really blessed our church with talented singers and musicians and he has touched us with the spirit of praise. When Bro. Daryl or Bro. Dean leads the choir in my favorites like, *Leave it All Behind*, I am transported in joy to the land that I desire and long for...HEAVEN! My Eternal Home where Jesus awaits! *Then Sings My Soul!* My soul reaches heavenward and with upraised hands and tear-filled eyes, I cry out to the One I love... Jesus, Jesus, Jesus.

Sometime God moves me to testify, and I feel what Moses must have felt, when he told the Lord that he was "slow of speech and slow of tongue". (Exodus 4:10) Sometimes my words won't come out! But God asks me to be faithful and obedient. So I stammer and falter and many times I can't complete my thoughts. But God is faithful, and he allows my words to be used to bless others and somehow they understand what I mean.

My dear friends thirst for what God has created in my soul for him! They must see the "heart" of my soul. Though I am weak in body and my sickness has taken away many of my abilities, the Almighty God of Heaven is using me! He uses me to praise Him; He uses my spirit gift to bless others to inspire others to keep on worshiping Him.

In 2 Cor.12:9-10, the apostle Paul rejoiced that his weakness had been used to bring more glory to Christ. If through my weakness God can bring more glory to His Son, then I say praise the Lord. Little is MUCH when God is in it

Thank You

I can't think of words bigger to say what is in my heart than THANK YOU!

To my family: Troy, Tondra and Rob, Rhonda and Scott, Kathy, Erin, Stan and Vickie, Dianne, Steve and family. I love you! You'll never know how your love and attention helped me. You prayed continuously that our Lord will see me through this and he did. We never know what God has in store for us. I'm just living each day to the fullest!

My Grandbabies: Levi, Gatlin and Devin Stetson, Channing, Canyon-- (It's God and you that got me through this).... THANK YOU...

To the doctors and nurses at Northeast Georgia Medical Center
Dr. James Parks, M.D.
Dr. Clinton Branch, Neurologist
To my doctors and nurses at Athens Regional Hospital
Dr. C. Van Morris, Neurologist
Dr. David M. Sailors, M.D.

Dr. Michael J. West, M.D.

Dr. Jerry Smith, Radiologist

To my doctors and nurses at Emory University Clinic

Dr. Jane Elmore, M.D.

Dr. Bradley Stern, M. D

To my Doctor and nurses at Duke University Medical Center

Dr. Allen H. Friedman , M.D.

My sister-in-law (sister really) ,Kathy, who sat with me all those times in the hospital and for helping take care of my grandkids. Kathy, thank you for staying with Mama Lois. She was a special person in my life. Thank you for telling her the truth! A few years later, she would say to me "You are a blessing from God in Heaven. You're a true miracle!! And I would say "Ain't God good"! I regret to say Mama Lois died in 2008.

My church family for everything! Every church for your prayers, visits, flowers, balloons, and other gifts! The telephone calls of love and concern! Your prayer chains with messages for others to pray for me. You prayed and I AM HERE!

The food everyone so graciously prepared to help Troy and the girls.

The ones that helped clean my house—Troy says bless you! The people that I worked with – thanks for everything. ...Especially for being patient with me. Especially to those of you who drove "Ms. Baba" Linda Anderson, who painted my house on the cover of this book.

Rev. Ralph O. Smith and Ms, Ruby, who stood by me. Becky Clough, who took all of my notes dating from 1968 to present and put them into a timeline and typed the first draft of my book.

God never leaves us nor forsakes. When I was at the end of my rope and was not sure how to continue with this book, God sent me two wonderful angels. I had prayed and prayed and prayed. One morning I woke up and I knew to call Carolyn Lineberger. I told her what I felt the Holy Spirit was directing me to do. I asked for her help to put everything together to complete the book. A great feeling of joy came over me when Carolyn agreed to help. She also volunteered her daughter, Amanda Davidson.

You're blessed when you're at the end of your rope. With less of you there is more of god and His rule. You're blessed when you feel you've lost what is most dear to you. Only then can you be embraced by the One most dear to you.
Matthew 5:3-4 The Message

Blessed are the poor in spirit: for theirs is the kingdom of heaven. Blessed are they that mourn: for shall be comforted.
Matthew 5:3-4 KJV

I tell you that if you on earth agree about anything you ask for, it will be one for you my My Father in heaven. For where two or three come together in My name, there am I with them.
Matthew 18:19-20 NIV

Again I say unto you, That if two of you shall agree on earth as touching any thing that they shall ask, it shall be done for them of my Father which is in heaven. For where two or three are gathered together in my name, there am I in the midst of them.
Matthew 18: 19-20 KJV

Personal note from Carolyn…"I did not know about the book. When Barbara asked me to help her, I knew I could not refuse. Barbara has s strong faith and is such a prayer warrior, that I knew I was supposed to work with her. I do not argue with the Holy Spirit."

I love all of you! It's been a long road. I don't know what lies ahead. But I have Jesus holding my hand. Keep me in your prayers, and keep the prayer chain going! Keep me on your church prayer list. Troy and I feel so unworthy. You all have been so good to us! We don't know what lies ahead, but I'm trusting in my Jesus as my Savior.

Thank you,
Troy & Barbara Jones

The A-B-C's of Salvation

Faith is a decision from your heart, which is demonstrated by authentic repentance and a changed life. Romans 10:9 says, "If you confess with your mouth, 'Jesus is Lord', and believe in your heart that God raised Him from the dead, you will be saved." If you would like to receive a new life through Jesus Christ, simply pray a prayer accepting Him and thanking Him for your new life. Visit a local church and become involved in living a Christ-like life and spreading the Good News of His love.

A-Admit you are a sinner. Repent, turning away from your sin. Romans 3:23 says "for all have sinned and fallen short of the glory of God."

B-Believe that Jesus is God's son and that He died on the cross for our sins. Romans 5:8 says, "but God proves His own love for us in that while we were still sinners Christ died for us."

C-Confess your faith in Jesus Christ as your personal Savior and Lord. Ephesians 2:8-9 says "For by grace you are saved through faith, and this is not from yourselves; it is God's gift – not from works, so that no one can boast."

If you have never trusted Jesus Christ as your Savior, pray with me this prayer.

Dear Christ Jesus, In all honesty I don't know how much I really want to change, but I know that I must. I can't do it myself. Here is my heart. Hear my earnest cry and look beyond my faults to my need. Forgive and heal me. I confess I do not keep your commandments. Nor do I truly follow your word but take this mess that I am and do your will with me. I open the door and invite God in as my Savior. Amen

Rev. James Duncan
2405 GA Hwy. 51 S
Lula, GA 30554

Mt. Carmel website www.mountcarmelbc.com
Rev. Duncan can be reached at 706-336-6988
Barbara Jones can be reached at littleismuch@yahoo.com

If my people, which are called by my name, shall humble
themselves, and pray, and seek my face, and turn from their
wicked ways; then will I hear from heaven, and will forgive
their sin, and will heal their land.

2 Chronicles 7:14 KJV